A LITTLE SPOT OF LIFE SKILLS & ACTIONS

Building Character
Educator's Guide

● HANDS-ON ACTIVITIES ● LESSON PLANS ● STEM ● WORKSHEETS

DIANE ALBER

DISCLAIMER

This guide is not for commercial use. You cannot resell or distribute any part of this guide for any form of compensation.

You may print up to 30 copies of the printables in the back of the guide to hand out to your class.

If you also purchased the PDF, it may NOT be distributed or shared with others.

If you would like to discuss school bulk discounts, print more copies, or use this guide in a class you charge for, please contact info@dianealber.com.

Check out more at www.dianealber.com

This guide is a companion to:

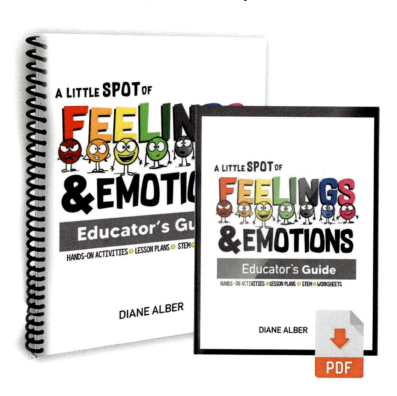

Copyright © 2021 Diane Alber All Rights Reserved. Printed in CHINA
All inquiries about this book can be sent to the author at info@dianealber.com
Published in the United States by Diane Alber Art LLC ISBN:978-1-951287-69-6
For more information or to book an event, visit our website: www.dianealber.com

ABOUT THE AUTHOR

Diane Alber has had a passion for art since she held her first crayon at age two, which inspired her to earn a Bachelor's in Fine Arts from Arizona State University. She is a wife and a mother of two young, energetic children, who love books. She was inspired to start writing and illustrating books because she saw a need for books that inspire art and creativity in children. Her series has evolved to cover topics that are hard to explain to children, like EMOTIONS, actions, and life skills. She hopes her series inspires creativity and encourages children to become the best they can be!

EDUCATOR TOOLS

We've heard from numerous educators, who sometimes feel like they are on an island with very little help in sight. That's why we created various Educator Tools. We spent months talking and listening to teachers, counselors, and those who homeschool about what they need to make teaching EMOTIONS, FEELINGS, ACTIONS, and LIFE SKILLS both educational and fun.

EDUCATOR GUIDES
(Lesson Plans, Hands-on Activities, and Worksheets)

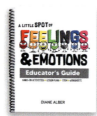 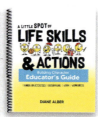

BOOKS

FLASHCARDS & STICKERS

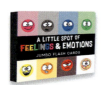 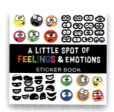 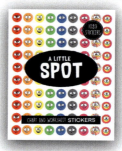

EDUCATOR TOOLS

PLUSH TOYS
3" Minis
8" BIG

PUPPETS

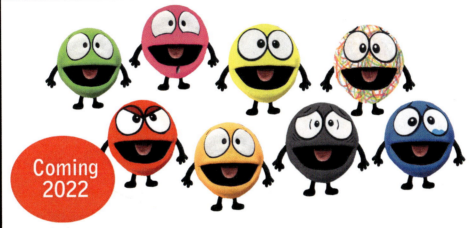

Coming 2022

LARGE INTERCHANGEABLE PILLOW CASES
24"

Coming 2022

CONTENTS

ACKNOWLEDGMENTS..12
INTRODUCTION TO SOCIAL-EMOTION LEARNING (SEL)..........13
HOW TO USE THIS BOOK..14
HOW ACTIONS AND FEELINGS WORK TOGETHER......................16
SCRIBBLE FEELINGS...18
FEELINGS ART...19
WHY USE SPOTS...20
EXPLAINING THE COLORS OF SPOTS...21
PLUSH TOYS..22
FEELINGS AND EMOTION FLASHCARDS....................................23
LARGE PILLOWS..24
5 WAYS TO USE LARGE PILLOWS..25
PUPPETS...26
7 WAYS TO USE PUPPETS...27
STICKERS..28
SPOT CHART STICKERS...29
GUIDE OUTLINE..30

● PART ONE: SOCIAL SKILLS..35
🟠 BELONGING...36
   Every Child Matters..36
   Belonging Name Plate..37
   Things In Common...39
   Get To Know You Bingo..39
   Conversation Catch..40

Feeling Included	41
⭕ DIVERSITY	42
Learning To Appreciate Differences	42
Just A Red Crayon	43
We All Shine	44
We Are All Apples	46
Kandinsky Apples	47
⭕ KINDNESS	44
Be Kind	48
Kind Apples	50
Kindness Pop-up Cards	51
Kindness By Giving	52
Kindness Through Thankfulness	53
⭕ TEAMWORK	54
Working As A Team!	54
Team Structure	56
Sneak Peek	57
Team Butter	60
We Support Each Other	62
Our Classroom As A Team	64
Splatter	66
Splatter Flowers	68
Collaborative Art	70
● EMPATHY	72
Empathy and Perspective	73
House or Crayon	75

PART TWO: RESPONSIBILE DECISION MAKING 77

SAFETY 78
Be Safe 78

RESPECT 80
Golden Rule 80

PATIENCE 82
Importance Of Patience 82
Kitchen Scraps Garden-Celery 83

HONESTY 84
Honesty Is The Best Policy 84
Tower Of Trust 85

RESPONSIBILITY 86
Responsibility In The Classroom 86
Decision Chart 86
Desk Chart 89

ORGANIZATION 90
Reduce Frustration And Save Time 90

PART THREE: SELF-AWARENESS 93

OPTIMISM 94
Learned Optimism 94
Lemonade In A Bag! 95
Push Out Negative Thoughts 96

PERSEVERANCE 98
Failure And Learning 94
Continued Drawing 99
Sock Throw 99
Carrot, Egg, or Cocoa 101

- COURAGE 102
  - Courage In Everyday Life 102
  - Courage Cards 103
- TALENT 104
  - Finding Your Way To Shine 104
  - My Talents 106
  - Talent Mobile 107
- CREATIVITY 108
  - Self-Expression 108
  - Creative Brain Break 109
- BOREDOM 110
  - Boredom Bubbles 111
- FLEXIBLE THINKING 112
  - Think Like A PALM TREE 112
  - Paper vs. Popsicle Stick 113
- FRUSTRATION 114
  - Cranky Students 114
  - Frustration Token 115
  - Mistake Poster 116

● APPENDIX: ACTIVITY RESOURCES 119
- GET TO KNOW YOU BINGO 120
- SIT OR STAND 121
- TEAM BUTTER 122-123
- TEAMWORK POSTER 124-125
- SNEAK PEEK SHAPES 126-127
- SPOT YOUR FEELINGS POSTER 128-131

TEAM HELPER	132-136
OUR SCHEDULE	137-144
KANDINSKY APPLES	145
SCRIBBLE SPOT	146
HOW DO YOU FEEL	147-148
MY TALENTS	149
PERSEVERANCE SOCK BUCKET	150
FIND THE EMOTION	151-152
WHO IS WHO	153-154
WHEN LIFE GIVES YOU LEMONADE	155
OPTIMISM	156-158
FRUSTRATION TOKEN	159
DECISION CHART	160
DAILY HOME SCHEDULE	161-163
NAME TAG	164-165
HOW TO MAKE A GOOD CHOICE	166-167
PERSONAL SAFETY INFORMATION	168
PRACTICE EMPATHY	169-170
PATIENCE	171
THANKFUL	172
TALENT MAP	173
COURAGE CARDS	174
SPOT YOUR EMOTION POSTER	175
GIVING	176-177
SPOT CHARTS	178-181
THINK SHEET	182

ADAPTING TO CHANGE	183
CUP DRAW YOURSELF	184
DID YOU MAKE A MISTAKE	187
PERSPECTIVE	188
FINISH THE PICTURE	189-193
KINDNESS POP-UP CARTS	194-195
TRAFFIC SIGNS	196
CONVERSATION CARDS	197
LAMP	198

ACKNOWLEDGMENTS

A big THANK YOU to everyone who has supported me! I am forever grateful to all the teachers, art teachers, parents, and caregivers who offered suggestions for new products, provided advice, and gave me the encouragement to keep creating. Thank you for spreading the word about my brand. Without you, none of this would have been possible!

A special thanks to Ashley, Amanda, Kristyna, Rachael, Hayley, Buddy, Erica, Rebecca, Julia, Adir, Karen, and Stacy for listening to my late-night ideas and offering fantastic advice.

I also want to thank my husband for believing in my ideas and letting me run with them! A big THANK YOU to my mom, who is the first to read every one of my books and looks forward to reading any new ones. And finally, thanks to my amazing children, who have inspired me to do everything in this book including all the worksheets and projects!

Diane Alber

INTRODUCTION TO SOCIAL-EMOTION LEARNING

Why teach SOCIAL-EMOTIONAL Learning?

SOCIAL-EMOTIONAL Learning (SEL) refers to the development of self-awareness, self-control, self-regulation, social skills, and responsible decision-making, all of which are essential for school and life success. In this guide, we focus on actions and skills that will help inspire and motivate children.

This guide will give you thought-provoking lessons, discussions, and activities to help your students identify ACTIONS and LIFE SKILLS. Students will learn how to develop self-control, a positive outlook, perseverance, and creative problem-solving skills for everyday tasks. Over several weeks, students will learn key ACTIONS and LIFE SKILLS to help them achieve more in the classroom and in life!

HOW TO USE THIS BOOK

This guide was created to help teach SOCIAL skills in SOCIAL-EMOTIONAL Learning. It is a companion to *A Little SPOT of Feelings & Emotions Educator Guide*. When both guides are used together, they offer a complete SEL curriculum. Each guide can be used on its own or in conjunction with one another. A gray box with the spiral-bound icon can be found when it's helpful to reference the *Feelings & Emotion Guide*.

Example:

For extended lessons on BELONGING and CONFIDENCE reference *Feelings & Emotions Guide* page 70-84

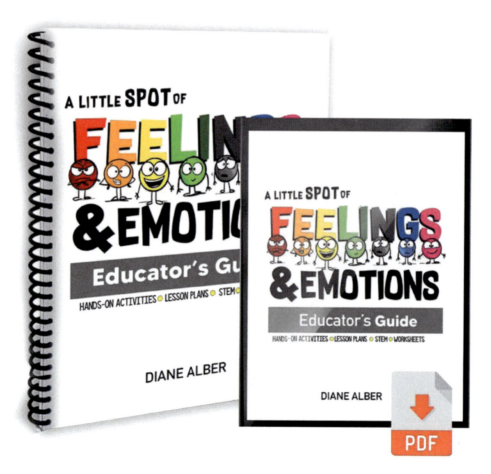

This guide is divided into three parts with supplementary activity sheets at the end. Each lesson or learning topic, refers to a children's picture book that reflects the respective section's content. The book icon indicates when the educator should be reading the book and what section to refer to.

Reference *Feelings & Emotions Guide*   Educator Reading   Discussion

Also included in each section is a hands-on arts and crafts activity, so students can play while they learn. This makes learning more meaningful and memorable. By using multiple senses, a student uses more of their brain, which leads them to be more engaged and retain more information. Puppet ideas and conversation are also recommended.

Hands-on: Worksheets   Hands-on: Arts and Crafts   Puppet   Learning Objective

We also included worksheets as an additional simple learning method that works well for distance learners. The worksheets can help with fine motor development and are beneficial for students with a short attention span. This Educator Guide was designed for both novice educators and those with years of classroom experience. Areas presented in red text are intended to serve as the Educator's script, if needed, for teaching the lesson.

HOW DO ACTIONS AND FEELINGS WORK TOGETHER?

This guide will mention FEELINGS and EMOTIONS often because FEELINGS and EMOTIONS motivate actions. For example, when a child learns how they are feeling, they can also understand how their feelings are tied to their actions. If a child knows what sadness is and can recognize sadness in others, it can motivate the child to try and help if they see sadness present in another fellow student.

If a child is experiencing frustration and their first reaction is to yell, once they learn how to manage their frustration, they can begin to control their response.

In both guides, we like to start with these two books:

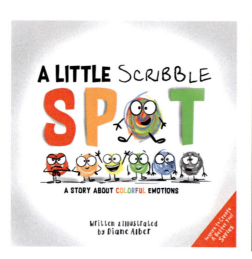
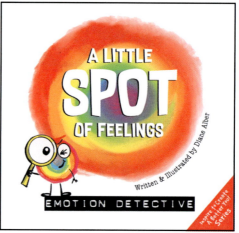

These books help with a brief overview of all the basic emotions and feelings that children often experience.

For extended lessons on overall Feelings and Emotions reference *Feelings & Emotions Guide* page 22-42

We recommend that teachers introduce feelings charts to their classes in phases, first presenting them and then incorporating them into their daily routines. After some time, students should utilize the charts on their own. Children should be able to independently move their names (or popsicle sticks, or photos, or magnets). This may occur as they enter the classroom for the first time each day. Teachers should encourage students to move their indicators as needed during the day.

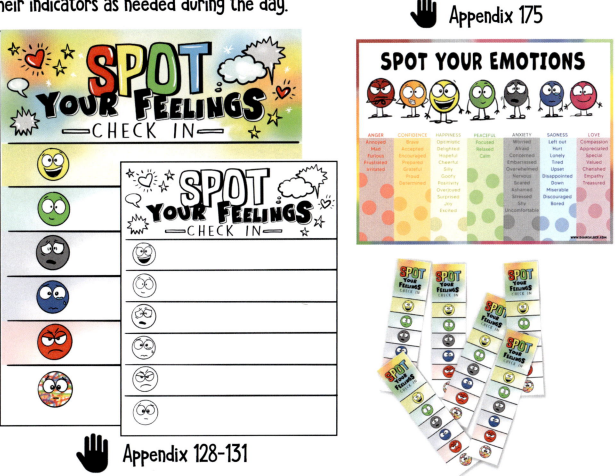

✋ Appendix 175

✋ Appendix 128-131

Having a feelings chart in the classroom can expose students to a wide range of emotions and emotional language. Try and incorporate emotional language in the classroom as much as possible. A great opportunity to do this is to associate characters with emotions when reading picture books. This method, combined with the introduction of our Peaceful Corner, has enabled students to recognize a wider range of emotions, particularly intense emotions, in themselves and others.

SCRIBBLE FEELINGS:

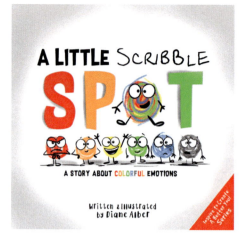

Materials needed:

- *A Little Scribble SPOT* to read to the class
- Scribble SPOT worksheet

Instructions:

While reading the book, *A Little Scribble SPOT*, have students create an EMOTION face every time SCRIBBLE SPOT meets a new EMOTION.

Appendix 146

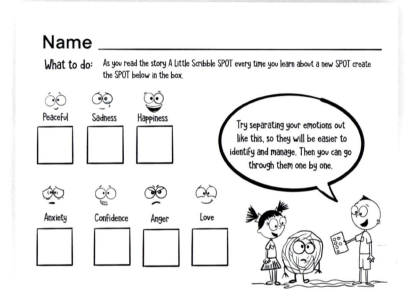

Copyright © 2021 Diane Alber www.dianealber.com *A Little SPOT of Life Skills & Actions Educator's Guide*. All Rights Reserved.

 Appendix 151-154

FEELINGS ART:

You can take it one step further and have students cut out their FEELING SPOTS to make a large classroom piece of art!

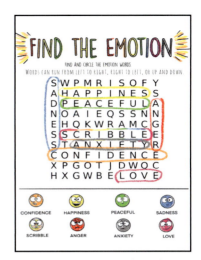

Thank you, Emily Shane, for the great idea! @art.teacher.thats.me

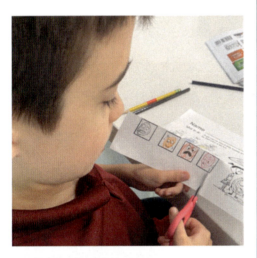

Copyright © 2021 Diane Alber www.dianealber.com *A Little SPOT of Life Skills & Actions Educator's Guide.* All Rights Reserved.

WHY USE SPOTS?

SPOTS are FUN and easy to visualize! When teaching a complex topic like PERSEVERANCE, KINDNESS, and RESPECT, having a little SPOT show you colorful illustrations of real-life situations with added guidance has been proven to be very successful.

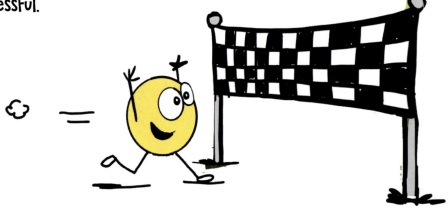

WHY ARE A LOT OF THE SPOTS YELLOW?

Occasionally we get asked why all the ACTION and LIFE SKILLS SPOTS are Yellow. This was done deliberately because we wanted students to associate these actions and life skills with HAPPINESS and JOY.

EXPLAINING THE COLORS OF THE SPOTS

We are constantly asked how we decided to choose the colors for each SPOT. The answer is simple: we based it on color psychology. Color can evoke emotion and communicate with a viewer; that is why it is often used in marketing and design. We felt it was important to follow color psychology as much as possible to benefit children in future careers.

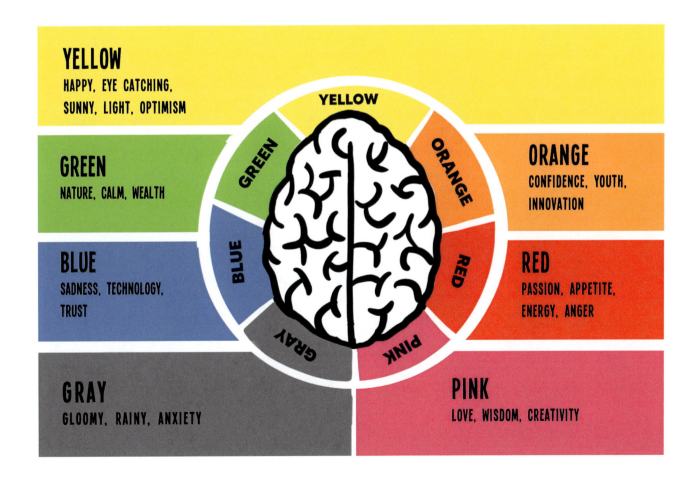

YELLOW — HAPPY, EYE CATCHING, SUNNY, LIGHT, OPTIMISM

GREEN — NATURE, CALM, WEALTH

BLUE — SADNESS, TECHNOLOGY, TRUST

GRAY — GLOOMY, RAINY, ANXIETY

ORANGE — CONFIDENCE, YOUTH, INNOVATION

RED — PASSION, APPETITE, ENERGY, ANGER

PINK — LOVE, WISDOM, CREATIVITY

PLUSH TOYS

We wanted plushies that could be used as a communication tool to encourage fun experiences and foster connection. If a student has a hard time verbally communicating, they can pick out the plushie that best represents how they FEEL. This adds another layer of teaching to help students retain more information.

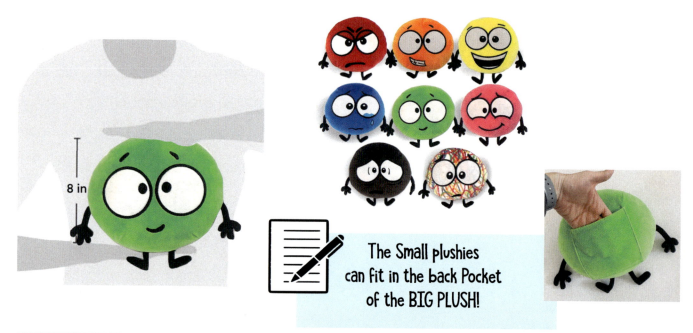

The Small plushies can fit in the back Pocket of the BIG PLUSH!

 For extended lessons on overall Feelings and Emotions reference *Feelings & Emotions Guide* page 22-42

FEELINGS AND EMOTION FLASH CARDS

 For GAMES with the FLASH CARDS reference *Feelings & Emotions Guide* page 13

We designed two different sizes of flashcards. The jumbo set can be used in a large group, classroom setting, or can be displayed on a board. The regular set is intended to be used for a smaller audience. It is great for a more personal experience or a smaller group (1-4 students). The regular set is wonderful for games and easier to store. We felt it was essential to include both sets to offer educators options.

The REGULAR Flashcards also fit great in a Pocket Chart that can hold 4" cards to make a FEELING CHART!

Appendix 147-148

LARGE PILLOWS

For extended lessons on a PEACEFUL SPOT room design reference *Feelings & Emotions Guide* page 44-51

5 WAYS TO USE THE LARGE PILLOWS

1) These pillow cases are designed to be interchangeable to save space in the classroom. Simply switch out the case with the SPOT of the lesson you are teaching that day!
2) They can be a perfect place to hold the big plush dolls!
3) They make great additions to any calming corner or reading nook!
4) They add lots of color for classroom decoration!
5) They can be used in a lesson as a visual to see how big a SPOT can grow.

PUPPETS

Puppets are some of the most cost-effective teaching tools in the classroom. Puppets have numerous advantages. They allow children to immerse themselves in a fantasy world making it easier for them to work out their emotions. Puppets are also a great visual aid for kids since puppets keep their attention and encourage them to participate in class. When children are having fun, they are more inclined to learn and embrace new knowledge.

Puppet: Look out for this icon for tips on how to incorporate puppets!

You can also make your own finger puppets using Crayola Model Magic and the feeling and emotion stickers!

7 WAYS TO USE PUPPETS

1) Use the CONFIDENCE, PEACEFUL, LOVE, and HAPPINESS SPOT to reinforce positive behavior. For example:
   *A puppet can join circle time, quiet time, or when the students are in centers and comment on how well the students are listening, writing, creating, etc.
   * A puppet can point out all the great things it sees children doing, like being kind.
2) Puppets can sing songs or help with phonics.
3) Puppets can be used to help with instruction and walk students through an activity.
4) Puppets can be used to role play examples of good behavior. For example:
   *When a student does something that another student doesn't like, like taking something without asking, the puppet would say, "Stop, I don't like it when you take the toy from me," and then the other puppet would say, "I'm sorry, here it is back."
5) Puppets can be used to make picture books come to life! They can be great to read to or used to tell stories.
6) Puppets can be used for public speaking, having the student use the puppet to tell the class something or recite a poem.
7) Puppets can be used to talk to when a child has a BIG emotion. Sometimes children have an easier time telling their emotions to puppets.

STICKERS

We have provided an easy self-contained art project. This SPOT sticker book is used several times throughout the guide, and it has enough stickers for an entire class. Each sticker sheet can be cut into quarters for easy distribution to students.

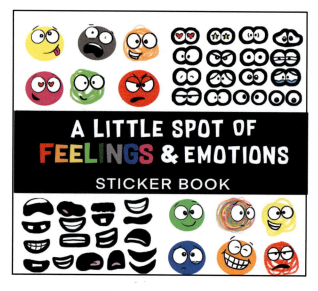

SPOT CHART STICKERS

We have heard and seen firsthand how beneficial sticker charts can be in motivating student's behavior.

These charts reinforce good behavior, making it more likely to happen again. They also allow you focus on positive behavior. This will help if you are feeling frustrated with a student. Each time your student does well, they can get a sticker in the spaces or stars on the chart. A certain number of stickers or stars adds up to a reward for your student.

Reward charts are a powerful way of:

- Encouraging behavior you want, like making a good choice, staying on task, hard work etc.
- Rewarding a student for practicing a new skill, like calming down an angry spot.

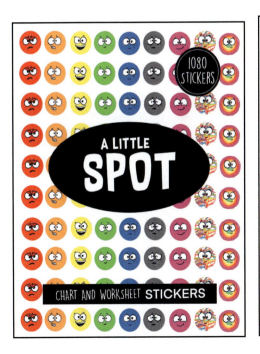

Appendix 178-181

GUIDE OUTLINE

Grade level(s): Kindergarten-2nd

This guide was created adhering to Common Core standards and CASEL: Effective Social-EMOTIONAL Learning Programs. It was developed to be a fun and creative resource to teach ACTIONS & LIFE SKILLS to elementary school students. The activities and lessons are created for 5-8 year olds but can easily be adapted for younger or older students.

ACTIONS & LIFE SKILLS

LEARNING OBJECTIVES

Students will:

- Identify similarities and differences between themselves and others.
- Learn how to develop positive relationships and communication skills.
- Identify, express, and describe their FEELINGS to themselves and others.
- Learn how to manage and self-regulate FEELINGS and EMOTIONS.
- Learn how to use color to express EMOTIONS.

The Educator might note that there is some repetition in the lessons and objectives; that was intended specifically to help reinforce key concepts.

TEACHING TIPS

Several steps can be taken to make this Educator Guide successful in the classroom:

- Read the lesson in its entirety before teaching the class.
- Use creativity and adapt to any lesson that would fit the classroom.
- Be inspiring to the students by motivating them and being positive.
- Model the new skills learned as often as possible in other subjects.

SEL (CASEL SEL FRAMEWORK)

● Concept 1: Self-Awareness
Students develop a sense of personal identity as they recognize the characteristics that make them unique as individuals. Students will start identifying FEELINGS in themselves and others. Students will also be able to develop a growth mindset and a sense of purpose.

● Concept 2: Social Awareness
Students will learn about perspective and practice seeing things from different perspectives. They will develop an awareness of their FEELINGS and the FEELINGS in others through daily interactions with peers and adults.

● Concept 3: Responsible Decision Making
Students will develop their curiosity and practice problem-solving. They will learn how to make good choices by developing flexible thinking skills.

● Concept 4: Relationship Skills
Students will develop the ability to communicate clearly and listen when needed, building connection and a sense of belonging with the class. Students will learn leadership skills and develop the skills needed to resolve conflict.

● Concept 5: Self-Management Skills
Students will learn managing and coping techniques. They will learn to demonstrate courage and initiative in everyday situations and develop self-discipline and self-motivation.

FINE ARTS (VISUAL ARTS STANDARDS)

● Concept 1: Create and Understand Visual Arts
Students will learn how to use a wide variety of materials to demonstrate personal interpretations of feelings, thoughts, and ideas.

ENGLISH LANGUAGE ARTS (COMMON CORE STANDARDS)

- **Concept 1: Key Ideas and Details**

Students will identify key details in stories and understand lessons.

- **Concept 2: Craft and Structure**

Students will start to identify unknown words that suggest FEELINGS or appeal to the senses.

- **Concept 3: Vocabulary**

Students will identify new meanings for familiar words, apply them accurately, and determine the meaning of unknown words.

- **Concept 4: Text Types and Purposes**

Students will use a combination of drawing and dictation to compose information.

SEL INTEGRATING MATH & SCIENCE (COMMON CORE STANDARDS)

Lesson plans will integrate discussion prompts and student reflection using various math and science projects to provide hands-on learning.

- **Concept 1: Geometry**

Students will learn how to identify and describe shapes as they create, compose, analyze, and compare shapes.

- **Concept 2: Science**

Students will learn states of matter.

NOTES:

NOTES:

PART ONE: SOCIAL SKILLS

- 🟠 BELONGING
- 🟡 TEAMWORK
- 🟡 DIVERSITY
- 🟡 KINDNESS
- 🟣 EMPATHY
- 🟡 THANKFUL

Learning and developing SOCIAL SKILLS can help prepare students in all aspects of their lives. Communicating effectively, working as a team, learning to appreciate others, and expressing empathy are all components of social skills.

TEACHING TIPS
- Establish expectations on behavior early in the school year.
- Be positive and become a role model for demonstrating SOCIAL SKILLS.
- During core subjects, look for opportunities to practice SOCIAL SKILLS.

 Reference *Feelings & Emotions Guide*
 Puppet
 Learning Objective
 Educator Reading
 Discussion
 Hands-on: Arts and Crafts
 Hands-on: Worksheets

Reminder: Areas presented in red text are intended to serve as the Educator's script, if needed, for teaching the lesson.

BELONGING

Every Child Matters!

Why is it essential to teach BELONGING? Needing to belong is very important to all of us. The need to BELONG starts with our initial caregiver and grows into adulthood. When children do not bond with their caregiver(s), studies show they will have lower self-esteem, a mistrust of people, and a more negative view of the world. The classroom can be a great place to start to boost a sense of belonging for every student.

Learning Objective:

Students will learn:
- How to make friends in a positive way
- Why it is important to be kind
- How to start a conversation
- The importance of names

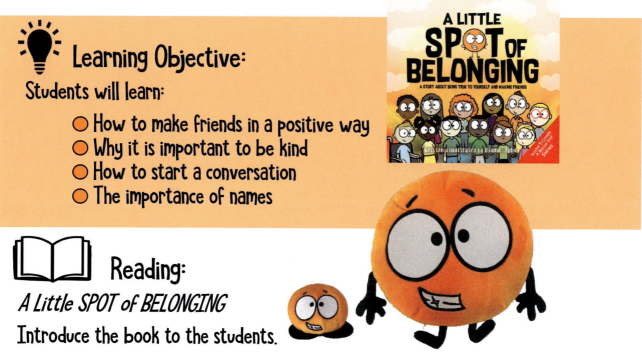

Reading:

A Little SPOT of BELONGING

Introduce the book to the students.

This book will help students learn about what it means to belong, and how we can help one another other feel accepted. Read the book. ***When reading, you can pass the plush around every time you read a new page, so everyone can make the plush belong!***

Reflect on the beginning of the book:
Belonging is the feeling you get when you have a great friend, when you are part of a group, or when you are part of a community that supports you.

Every human on this planet wants to feel like they belong somewhere, and we all have the power to help each other belong! Kindness is a huge part of belonging. Kindness makes others feel good, and it helps you build friendships.

Did you know that NAMES are so important in helping someone feel important? Names are how people can remember us after meeting, and it's how someone can get our attention or identify us. When someone remembers your name, it can make you feel special. Today we are going to make BELONGING SPOT name art!

Belonging Name Plate

Appendix 164-165

Materials Needed:
- Circle Sheet
- Name Plate Printable
- Crayons
- Glue

Print the Circle Sheet on orange paper and have the students write their names, with each circle representing one letter in their name. Have them glue the circles on the name plate.

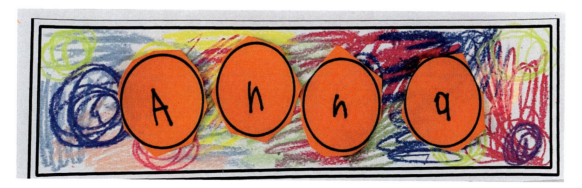

BELONGING (cont.)

📖 **Reflect back to:** That's why BELONGING needs to start with you, first! What are some things we can do that can help build our CONFIDENCE SPOT? Saying positive words about ourselves?

 For additional lessons on CONFIDENCE SPOT reference *Feelings & Emotions Guide* page 70

📖 **Reflect back to:** Asking questions is another great way to show someone that you want to be their friend. When you ask questions, it gives you a chance to build a connection. You might even find something in common!

 **Discussion:**

Discuss the importance of being part of a group or family and how it feels to be a part of something.

What are some things that we all have in common in this class?

Are we all students?

Are we all here to learn?

We can make this class a place where we can make everyone feel like they belong.

Finding things in common with someone else is a great way to start a connection. When you ask questions, it shows someone that you want to know more about them, and you are friendly.

We are going to play a game that will help you see how much you have in common with other kids in the class.

✋ Things In Common

Materials Needed:

🟠 Sit or Stand printout

Project the worsheet to the class. Now go through every line and have the kids sit or stand depending on how they would answer the question.

 Appendix 121

📖 **Reflect back to:** CONVERSATIONS can be a little tricky sometimes because they require TEAMWORK. Think of a CONVERSATION like a game of catch. What are some questions that would be great to ask? Asking questions like, "What are you doing this summer?" or "I just love when it rains, do you like the rain?" starts a connection. This type of conversation is called "small talk," and it's a great way to start a conversation.

✋ Get to know you BINGO

Materials Needed:

🟠 BINGO printout

Hand out the BINGO worksheet to the class. Have them find other students that have the same interests as them.

 Discussion:

How did it feel when you found something in common with someone else?

 Appendix 120

BELONGING (cont.)

Conversation Catch

Materials Needed:
- Ball or Confidence SPOT

When the ball is tossed, ask a question. Like, "What did you do this weekend?"

When the ball is caught, answer the question. Like, "I went to the park!"

Now TOSS the ball back and ask a question. Like, "What did YOU do this weekend?"

When the ball is caught, answer the question. Like, "I went swimming."

If kids are having trouble with what to ask, you can use these conversation questions and have the students draw them out of a jar!

Appendix 197

Step One: Have the students pair up, and have them practice by tossing a ball or SPOT to each other.

Step Two: When the ball is tossed ask a question. Like, "What did you do this weekend?"

Step Three: When the ball is caught, answer the question. Like, "I went to the park".

Step Four: Toss the ball back and repeat Step 2.

Feeling Included

It's important to identify the children that are having a difficult time socially as soon as possible. This can be done by asking the children several times during the year to write down three friends they want to work with or be paired with. As you review their choices, you will be able to identify what children are rarely chosen. Try and pair those students with children that are more socially developed and kind.

Discussion:
Discuss how it feels to be included and left out. What are some things you can do to connect with someone? (For example: Remember their name.)

It is also great to see who your students are connecting with from a faculty perspective. You can do this by printing out pictures of the faculty on one sheet of paper. Have each student circle the teachers or staff who they feel like they could talk to if they needed help. If you notice a child has circled very few people, you can share with other faculty and ask others to help reach out to that child and say hello. It's great to do this at the beginning of the year and the end to see how it changes.

 For extended lessons on BELONGING and CONFIDENCE reference *Feelings & Emotions Guide* page 70-84

DIVERSITY

Learning To Appreciate Differences

Children learn early on from interactions, books, tv, photographs that their peers have a variety of abilities, languages, and backgrounds. It's natural to notice similarities and differences and be curious, but we want to encourage children to appreciate differences rather than fear them. We want to create an environment where it's okay to ask questions and learn about others.

Learning Objective:

Students will learn:
- To appreciate uniqueness
- To build a positive identity
- To appreciate individuality

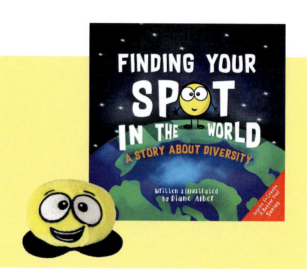

 Reading:

Finding your SPOT in the World. This book will help you learn how your differences make you unique, and how the world needs them. Do you know what DIVERSITY means? Diversity means different types of things or people being included in something, like a classroom.

Just A Red Crayon

Before reading the book, hand out a RED crayon to each person in the class and a piece of paper and say: Okay, draw a rainbow! They should all look at you puzzled and wonder how they will do that with just one color. Now give them orange and ask, Okay, can you draw a rainbow now? What other colors do you need to draw a rainbow? And proceed to hand out those colors.

 Now begin reading the book. Read to: If everyone were the same, that wouldn't be fun at all. Imagine only having the same color crayon in the crayon box? How could you create a beautiful rainbow? That's why I'm here to help you discover what makes you unique and how we can all grow together.

💬 Discussion:

Discuss how people come in all shapes and sizes with different abilities and backgrounds. What does it mean to be unique? What are some things that make you you unique?

Discuss how being an artist, dancer, singer, are all things that that can make you unique.

DIVERSITY

 We All Shine

Materials Needed:
- Worksheet
- Name Plate Printable
- Flashlight
- (Optional) Scrap book paper

 Puppet:

Have the puppet go around the room and comment on all the artwork being created! An example would be: "I love your use of shapes and color."

Hand out the worksheet and ask every student to color it. As they color talk about how every lamp looks different though, they all have one thing in common. They light up any room!

Now grab a flashlight and turn it on. The light of the lamp is the most important part of the lamp. This is like a person's heart. So regardless of what their lamp looks like, they all can shine!

 **Discussion:**

 Appendix 198

Discuss how we are like lamps. We may all look different on the outside, but we all can bring light to the world with our kindness, courage, perseverance, honesty, and generosity. Point out the various designs the students are using as they design their lamps.

What are some ways you can shine? Being kind, being thankful, being honest, etc.

NAME:

WE MIGHT LOOK LIKE DIFFERENT LAMPS

BUT WE CAN ALL LIGHT UP A ROOM!

 Another version with scrapbook paper!

Copyright © 2021 Diane Alber www.dianealber.com *A Little SPOT of Life Skills & Actions Educator's Guide.* All Rights Reserved.

DIVERSITY

 ## We Are Like Apples

Materials Needed:
- Every student needs an apple

Instructions:

Step One: Give each student an apple or have them bring one to class.

Step Two: Direct the students to examine their apples carefully. They will need to be able to recognize their apple later.

Step Three: Collect all the apples and line them up, making sure the students don't know whose is whose.

Step Four: Direct each person to find their apple. When everyone has found their apple have them return to their desks.

Step Five: Have the students explain how they knew the apple was theirs.

Step Six: Make a point to discuss these unique features of the apples and point out that each of us has unique features, too.

💬 Discussion:

What if everyone had the exact same apple? Could you tell yours apart? Did you know that there are over 8,000 different varieties of apples? They are also grown on different trees; some are full size, and some are very small trees that only grow 8-10 ft tall.

🖼️ Kandinsky Apples

We are going to make the most unique and colorful apples. We are going to use a technique that Kandinsky used in his circle paintings.

Appendix 145

✏️ TEACHING TIP: Search Wassily Kandinsky on the internet to find an image of "Kandinsky Circles." This also offers a great opportunity to teach your students about a famous painter as well.

KINDNESS

Be Kind

Most people have heard the phrase "random acts of kindness," which refers to a selfless act of giving that results in the happiness of another person. In addition to bringing joy to another person, children who show kindness increase their ability to form strong connections, which leads to a higher peer acceptance rate. Kindness is more then just "being nice to someone;" it's a skill that needs to be taught, reinforced, and rewarded.

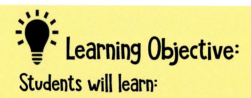 **Learning Objective:**

Students will learn:
- What it means to be kind
- How to help one another
- How kindness can grow

 Reading:

A Little SPOT of Kindness

Introduce the book to the students. Do you know what the word KINDNESS means? This book will help show us ways that we can be kind!

A SPOT of kindness has a sticky back. The reason my back is sticky is so I can help kindness stick to you!

 Reflect on the beginning of the book:

Did you know that every time you are kind, a layer of happiness is added to your heart and to the hearts of others? And since you both have the power to make good choices, you can start making a choice to be KIND!

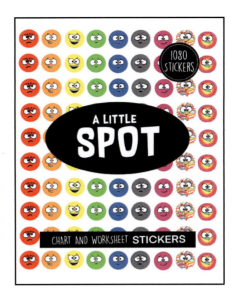

💬 Discussion:

What are some ways you can be kind? How do you feel when someone is kind to you? Can you think of a time that someone was kind to you?

 For extended lessons on kindness and happiness reference *Feelings & Emotions Guide* page 87-89, 97

KINDNESS

✋ Kind Apples

Materials Needed:
- Two Apples

💬 Discussion:

How do both apples look on the outside? How do they look on the inside? When people say hurtful things, we can look okay on the outside, but on the inside we are hurting. Can you think of the last time someone said something hurtful to you? How did it feel?

Instructions:

Step One: Before class, you need to drop one of the apples on a counter. It takes over one hour to bruise. Make sure not to brusie the apple too much; it needs to look unharmed on the outside.

Step Two: Show the students two apples. Then proceed to say mean things to one apple and nice things to another.

Step Three: Cut open the apples to reveal the bruised apple that had been treated unkindly.

 # Kindness Pop-Up Cards

Instructions:

Have the students think of kind words and write them on a board to inspire the students' talking bubbles. Color and cut out the sheets!

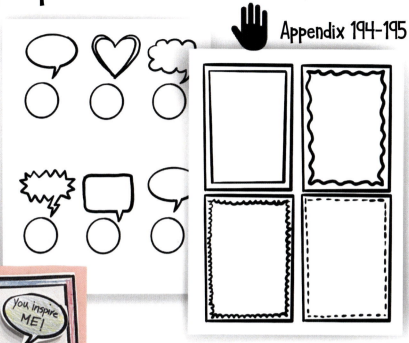

Appendix 194-195

Thank you Emily Shane for the great idea! @art.teacher.thats.me

Create a small paper accordion that looks like a "Z" to attach characters and talking bubbles with tape to create the pop-up effect!

KINDNESS

Kindness By Giving

Being kind is more than saying nice things. It's about giving and being thankful too! When children participate in actions that benefit those less fortunate than themselves, they gain a real sense of perspective and learn to be thankful for things they have.

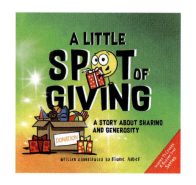

 Reading:

A Little SPOT of Giving

Introduce the book to the students. Do you know what giving means? Giving is caring for someone else, being helpful, and being kind.

Discussion: Model some examples of giving. This could be donating your time to people in need, or helping someone, etc. How did it feel when someone gives you something? How does it feel when you give something to someone else?

Appendix 176-177

Kindness Through Thankfulness

Teaching children to be thankful doesn't have to be complicated. Children will learn from others around them. If you and the students are becoming more thankful for everyday things, it will start to spread within your classroom. When you are thankful for people around you, kindness grows as well.

 Reading:

A Little Thankful SPOT

Introduce the book to the students. Do you know what the word Thankful means? Being thankful means you are happy for what you have, who you are, and what you have done.

 Discussion:

Model some examples of some things you are personally thankful for. This could be your home, children, pets, etc. Then ask the class: What are you thankful for?

 Puppet:

Have the puppet go around the room and say what he's thankful for and why. An example could be, "I'm thankful for these books, so I can read to you!"

 Appendix 172

TEAMWORK

Working As A Team!

Teamwork requires essential social skills. Children will need to learn how to cooperate, problem solve, communicate, listen, and create to be successful in life. When working as a team, children will learn the importance of individual roles and listening as a cohesive unit. Teamwork can improve children's self-confidence, reduce bullying, and build strong support systems. Almost all career paths involve people working closely with one another, and the benefits of teamwork will extend far outside the classroom to help students in the future.

 Learning Objective:

Students will learn:
- ○ Importance of clear communication
- ○ Leadership skills
- ○ Conflict Resolution
- ○ How to work as a team

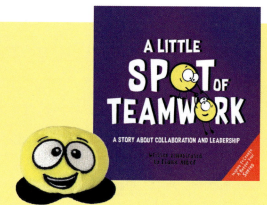

 Reading:

A Little SPOT of Teamwork

Introduce the book to the students. Do you know what the word TEAMWORK means? This book will help you learn about what it means to belong and help each other feel accepted.

Reflect on the beginning of the book: A TEAM is two or more individuals working together to achieve a common goal. You might see a pair of people working together, a crew, or even a large group! Discuss different types of teams, sports teams, project teams, etc.

📖 Reflect on the book: In TEAMWORK, you COLLABORATE a lot! COLLABORATION is when you have a group of people with a lot of different talents and skills working together to create something amazing!

💬 Discussion:

How is this classroom a team?

Name an activity that we have done as a class that showed teamwork?

What makes a good team? Discuss the poster below.

Teamwork Poster

Talk about all the different ways we can show TEAMWORK. Have them color this poster as you discuss.

✋ Appendix 124-125

TEAMWORK

Team Structure

A team is usually constructed of a Leader and Helpers (teammates). You need both to have a successful team. Every role of the team is important. A teammate is just as important as a leader. Without one, it would be very difficult for the team to be successful. Let's look at the responsibility of each role.

 Reflect on the book

LEADER: A LEADER'S job is to guide the TEAM to their goal through clear COMMUNICATION. They can recognize the strengths and weaknesses of the TEAM and make sure everyone stays on track. They are also good at ENCOURAGING the TEAM and resolving conflicts.

TEAMMATE: A TEAMMATE'S job is to follow the LEADER and do their part. They can do this by LISTENING, WORKING HARD, and having a POSITIVE ATTITUDE.

 Discussion:

Can you think of a good Leader? Why do you think that a Leader is a good leader? Maybe a principal, teacher, parent, coach, or captain?

Can you think of a good team? Maybe a sports team? What do you think makes a good team?

We are going to play a game that requires leadership. Leadership involves good communication skills, the ability to give direction and follow instruction. These skills are needed for leaders and teammates alike to form a good team.

# Sneak Peek

Materials Needed:

○ Two print outs

 Remind students that the goal is for the LEADER to communicate as CLEARLY and KINDLY as possible to help their team, and for the TEAMMATES to listen and follow instructions.

Before Activity:

The Educator cuts out the design cards and shapes. Place just the shapes in the envelope for each team. Place students in teams. Assign a Leader for each team.

TEACHING TIP:

This activity is also great when teaching SHAPES!

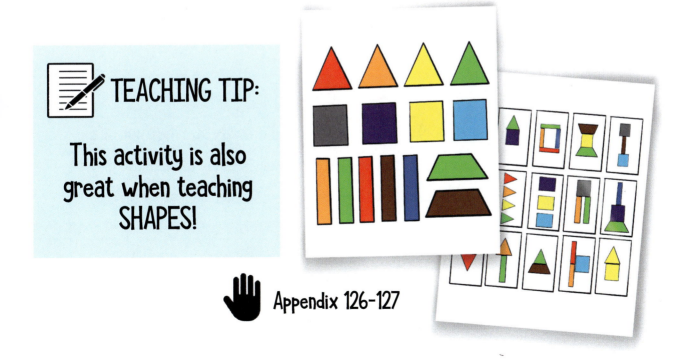

Appendix 126-127

TEAMWORK

Instruction:

Step One: Have the leaders of each team look at the design the Educator has chosen and try to memorize it before returning to their team. (Be careful not to reveal the design to the teammates)

Step Two: The leader must go back to the team and instruct them how to put together the design. The team has one minute to build a replica of the design without the leader touching any of the pieces.

Step Three: If, after one minute, no team has successfully built a replica, the leaders are allowed another sneak peek. This will continue until a team has completed the design successfully.

Step Four: Rotate leaders until everyone has had a chance to be a leader.

TEACHING TIP:

Listen to how the teams are working together and take notes on what you see working. For example, you saw a team call out all the shapes by name first like, "we need to use one red triangle, one orange square, and one yellow triangle."

After the activity go over all the notes you collected and share them with the class.

📝 TEACHING TIP:

If the designs provided are too easy or too hard, feel free to make your own designs and shapes. This also makes for a great lesson in GEOMETRY!

💬 Discussion:

What was the hardest part of being a leader?
What was the most challenging part of being a teammate?
What would you try differently next time?
Was there conflict? How did you resolve the conflict?

TEAMWORK

📖 Reflect on the book:

COOKING is so much fun as a TEAM. DINNER TIME is another time when everyone can do their part and work together. There are several tasks to do. You can set the table, clean off the dirty dishes, clean the table, and sweep the floor. It's a little hard to cook in the classroom, but I thought it would be fun to make BUTTER!

✋ Team BUTTER

✋ Appendix 122

Materials Needed:
- Heavy Cream
- Baby Food Jar
- Salt
- Crackers
- Worksheet
- Ice

Instruction:

Step One: Fill the jar halfway with cream and salt (salt is optional).

Step Two: The Jar needs to be shaken for at least 10 minutes, so if you have 20 students, each student will need to shake the jar for 45 seconds. Have them pass the jar until the cream separates into a lump of butter and buttermilk.

Step Three: Have the educator remove the buttermilk and add an ice cube to help rinse the butter and harden it even further.

Step Four: Spread on crackers or bread for the class to enjoy! Make sure you refrigerate it!

Discussion:

How would it feel to be the only one having to shake the butter?

What if you didn't have a leader helping give directions?

 Appendix 123

 **TEACHING TIP:**

This activity also goes great when teaching States of Matter!

TEAMWORK

We Support Each Other!

Just like in the Team Butter activity, if only one person had to shake the butter all by themselves, that would be an exhausting task for one person. That is what is wonderful about TEAMWORK. We all can support each other. Sometimes in our lives, we will need others to help us.

Materials Needed:
- 17 Red Solo Cups or paper cups
- Strong cardboard or board

SUPPORT EACH OTHER!

Step 1: Place one solo cup on the ground and try and stand on it. The cup will crush immediately

Sometimes there will be a situation when you need someone's help. This single cup couldn't handle all the weight alone.

Step 2: Place 16 cups as close together as possible. On top place strong cardboard. It should hold your weight easily.

With the help of other cups you are supported!

 Discussion:

Discuss what it means to be supported. How can you support others? Can you think of a time when you needed help? What are some situations you can remember of where it was great to have a team around you? (Maybe your family supporting you? Or a classroom that believed in you?)

 Appendix 184

TEAMWORK

Our Classroom Is A TEAM

You will be blessed with a group of students for around nine months. During this time, if you create a safe, loving, and caring environment, it will provide the best place for your students to learn. Treating your students like you are all part of TEAM is the first step in helping them feel like they BELONG, have a purpose, and feel valued in the classroom.

📖 **Reflect on the book:** In school, there are a lot of TEAMS! Not only can students COLLABORATE during projects, but they can also share tasks like opening the door, changing the weather chart, or turning off the lights. And you can switch up the tasks every week, so everyone can participate and help out the teacher!

You can discuss the current jobs you have created for the class and the importance of each job.

 **Discussion:**

What is a job we could add to the board?

What is the importance of us all doing our part and completing our jobs?

 Appendix 138-141

I'm the WEATHER CHANGER. I'm in charge of updating the weather on this chart!

I'm the LINE LEADER!

I'm the DOOR HOLDER!

TEAMWORK

Splatter

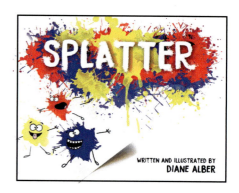

 Reading:

Splatter
Introduce the book to the students.
This book will help you learn about what it means to work as a team!

 Reflect on the beginning of the book: But this crew was different from most that you'd see, they each worked alone, not together as three. One color per drawing is how they'd each play, never knowing there would be a much better way. Are there things that you would prefer to do by yourself? Are their times when working alone is better?

 Discussion:

There are three main colors in this book: RED, YELLOW, and BLUE. Do you know what these colors are called? Primary colors. When primary colors mix they can make secondary colors.

What did RED, YELLOW and BLUE paint? What would you paint with RED, YELLOW and BLUE?

What changed in the book that convinced RED, YELLOW and BLUE to finally try working together? Can you name a time when working together as a team was better?

Have you ever made art with others? Side walk chalk, murals, scupltures, etc.

How did RED help the team persevere? He used positive words to keep the team going.

COLOR WHEEL

PRIMARY COLORS

RED   YELLOW   BLUE

SECONDARY COLORS

ORANGE   GREEN   VIOLET

IF YOU MIX EQUAL PARTS OF TWO PRIMARY COLORS YOU WILL GET A SECONDARY COLOR.

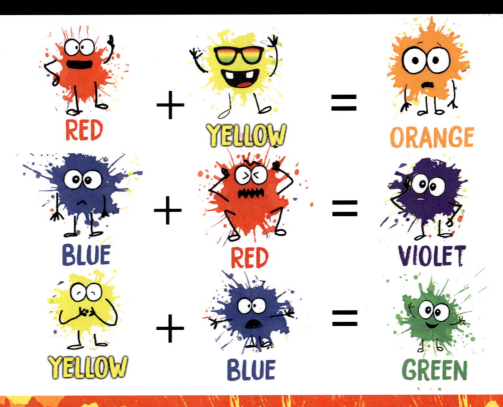

RED + YELLOW = ORANGE

BLUE + RED = VIOLET

YELLOW + BLUE = GREEN

Splatter Flowers

Materials Needed:
- Salad Spinner
- Acrylic or tempera paint
- Paper

Step One: Place a small piece of paper in the bottom of the salad spinner.

Step Two: Add paint. Try and drizzle the paint and avoid making a giant blob in the center.

Step Three: Spin the salad spinner!

TEACHING TIP: If the students make one big giant blob of paint in the middle, spread it out slightly with a straw before you spin, so it spreads evenly.

○ Add some emotion SPOT stickers to make them come to life!

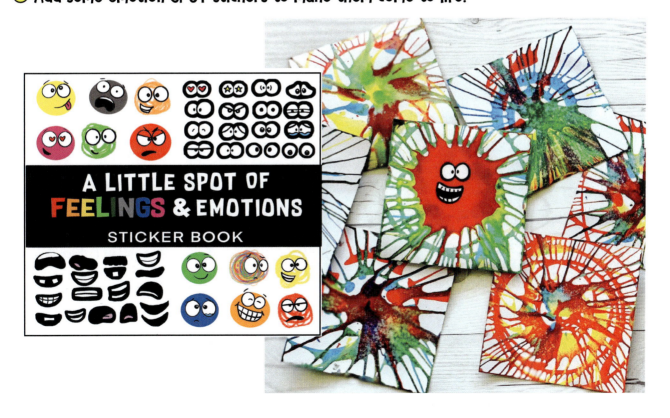

TEAMWORK

Collaborative Art

Art is a great way for students to grow their team-building skills. Collaborative art focuses on cooperation rather than competition. Students will learn from each other through the process of creating. They have to make choices and rely on each other's strengths. Students will learn to respect each other's skill sets, and they will each be able to bring home a piece of artwork that was made by a TEAM.

Examples:

Reflect on the book: Sure, you could make art by yourself, but you will learn so much more when you work as a TEAM! By making one big giant portrait, you can practice problem-solving by figuring out what design to do together, learn new techniques from your TEAMMATES, and create new art that you would not have thought of yourself! Are there past books we have read that had characters that had strong emotions? Do colors make you FEEL emotions?

Materials Needed:

- A piece of paper for every student
- Crayons, markers, color pencils

Instruction:

Explain to the students that everyone is going to be contributing to each other's art pieces. They will each have 20 seconds to add some artwork to their sheet, and the goal is to make a circle design. Then they will pass the art to the left. Show the class some of the examples.

 TEACHING TIP:

If you did the activity on page 17 of this guide, you can reference how this is another version of collaborative art.

EMPATHY

Empathy And Perspective

Empathy is a form of communication. It demonstrates that you are aware of what someone is going through, even if you don't comprehend how it feels to them. Empathy says, "I want you to know that I'm here to listen, you're not alone, and I'd like to understand how you are feeling."

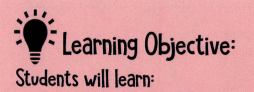

Learning Objective:
Students will learn:
- What it means to see things from a different perspective
- How to show empathy

Puppet:
You can use the LOVE puppet to role-play situations on what you could say to show empathy!

 **Reading:**
A Little SPOT of Empathy
Introduce the book to the students.
Do you know what Empathy means? Empathy is being able to understand and share feelings with someone else.

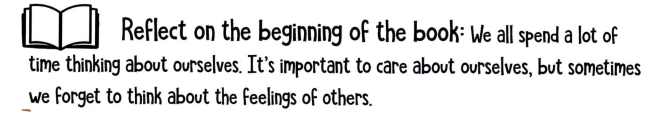

Reflect on the beginning of the book: We all spend a lot of time thinking about ourselves. It's important to care about ourselves, but sometimes we forget to think about the feelings of others.

Consider the following scenario: Your student yells in frustration at the project they are working on. You are also frustrated because this is the third time this week this has happened, so you firmly explain to the child that this behavior is not okay.

Your reaction is understandable. You don't want to disrupt the class, and your student needs to learn strategies to help manage frustration. However, reacting with frustration puts the focus on how YOU feel rather than on what's happening with your student, who may be struggling. Empathy has the power to change the dynamic. It allows you to recognize not only what YOU see and feel, but also what your student is going through.

Discussion:

Discuss situations where you could show empathy. Maybe a new student comes to school or a child just lost a pet. What could you say to them?   Appendix 169-170

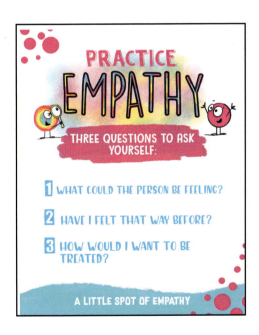 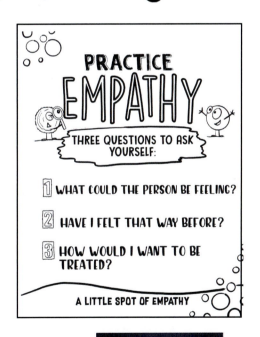

 For extended lessons on EMPATHY and SADNESS reference *Feelings & Emotions Guide* page 62-65

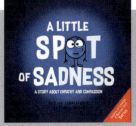

EMPATHY

📖 Reflect on the begining of the book: For example, look at this picture. Both of you are looking at the exact same thing, but you are each seeing something different. That means you have different PERSPECTIVES.

💬 Discussion:

Discuss different scenarios where people could have a different perspective of a situation. Maybe someone is playing tag, but the person tagged feels like they were hit.

 House Or Crayon?

Materials Needed:
- Perspective worksheet

 **Puppet:**
You can use the LOVE puppet to explain the instructions of the worksheet.

Instructions:

Step One: Pass out the worksheet to the students and explain that they need to decide whether they think this image is a house or crayon. They need to color the sheet of paper and write their answer on the line below.

Step Two: Collect all the papers and take a tally of how many papers said House and how many papers said Crayon.

 Appendix 188

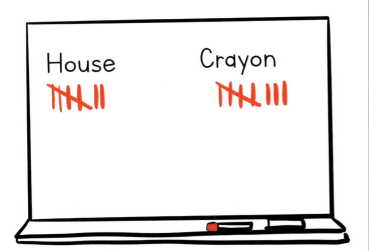

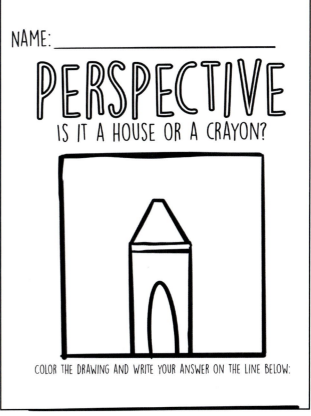

 **Discussion:**
Discuss how the class had different perspectives or all shared the same perspective.

Copyright © 2021 Diane Alber www.dianealber.com *A Little SPOT of Life Skills & Actions Educator's Guide.* All Rights Reserved.

NOTES:

PART TWO: RESPONSIBLE DECISION MAKING

- SAFETY
- RESPONSIBILTY
- ORGANIZATION
- RESPECT
- PATIENCE
- HONESTY

Learning and developing the ability to make positive choices can help prepare students in all aspects of their lives. Being able to consider consequences of a potential decision is key in learning how to build stronger relationship and learn more effectively.

TEACHING TIPS
- Acknowledge when children are making GOOD CHOICES
- Be positive and become a role model for demonstrating SOCIAL SKILLS
- During core subjects, look for opportunities to practice SOCIAL SKILLS

 Reference *Feelings & Emotions Guide*   Puppet   Learning Objective  Educator Reading   Discussion  Hands-on: Arts and Crafts   Hands-on: Worksheets

Reminder: Areas presented in red text are intended to serve as the Educator's script, if needed, for teaching the lesson.

SAFETY

Be Safe

The feeling of being safe is important for everyone, and it's possible to teach safety to children without scaring them. By teaching children the importance of being safe you empower them with the knowledge to avoid harmful situations for themselves or others. Being safe not only makes a better environment for them but for their peers as well.

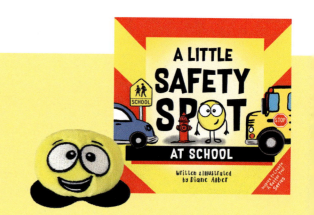

 Learning Objective:

Students will learn:

- ○ The importance of safety
- ○ What to do if they see bullying
- ○ The importance of safety drills

 Reading:

A Little Safety SPOT

Introduce the book to the students.

Do you know what it means to feel safe?

 Reflect on the beginning of the book: It is important that we are SAFE when we learn, play, and have fun! The other SAFETY SPOTS and I are here to show you how you can be SAFE AT SCHOOL!

 **Discussion:**

Discuss situations at home, in the classroom, and on the playground where students can practice being safe. Have you ever been in an unsafe situation? What did you do? Can you think of things in this classroom that we practice safely every day? Scissors? Washing our hands? Looking for signs?

Did you know there is a whole organization that helps create safety and health rules for the workplace called OSHA (Occupational Safety and Health Administration)? Did you know that colors of signs play an important role? OSHA determined these color code standards that will be helpful to know when you are looking at signs:

Red: Indicates HIGH DANGER that could happen quickly.
Yellow: Indicates caution. Be aware of your surroundings to avoid things like tripping or falling.
Orange: Indicates construction or warning. Be aware of your surroundings. Are you in danger of being hurt by an object or chemicals?
Blue: Indicates information about an item or area.
Black and White: Indicates information about guiding traffic or telling people where to go.

 Appendix 196

Appendix 168

 **Discussion:**

Discuss why it is important to know your personal safety information.

RESPECT

Golden Rule

One of the most crucial traits a child can practice is respect. Teaching children to respect others will foster positive interactions with their family, friends, and community for the rest of their lives. Respect may be instilled in children in various ways, but at the end of the day, it's about making sure they treat people the way they want to be treated.

 Learning Objective:

Students will learn:
- What it means to be respectful
- How they can be respectful in the classroom

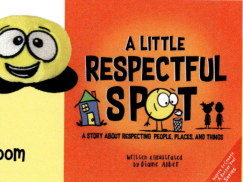

 Reading:

A Little Respectful SPOT

Introduce the book to the students.

Do you know what RESPECT means? This book will help show us what it means to be RESPECTFUL.

Reflect on the beginning of the book: Being RESPECTFUL tells people you not only care about them, but you care about yourself, too! And today, I'm going to show you examples of how you can RESPECT PEOPLE, PLACES, and THINGS! What are some things we already do that are respectful every day? (Taking care of school supplies, walking in the halls, and listening to the teacher.)

 Discussion:

Discuss situations at home, in the classroom, or on the playground where students can use their skills to respect each other.

How can you show RESPECT to PEOPLE? By saying "Please and Thank you?" What about following instructions, raising your hand, and waiting your turn when someone else is speaking? How about giving others personal space and being patient?

How can you show RESPECT to PLACES? By placing trash in a garbage can? By walking on sidewalks and not through grass or flowers? How about not making a mess on walls or running in the hallways?

How can you show RESPECT to THINGS? When you are done with something, put it away. Handle supplies carefully and ask someone to use something before taking it.

 Appendix 187

 Puppet:

Have the puppet talk about being respectful. For example, "I can be respectful to my classmates by listening to them."

PATIENCE

Importance Of Patience

It's very important to help teach children patience. Not only will they learn how to stay calm in stressful situations, but it will help prevent them from becoming frustrated when things aren't happening as quickly as they would like. There will be numerous situations in your classroom where you will need children to be patient. For example, while you help out another student, prepare for a project, or transition to a new lesson.

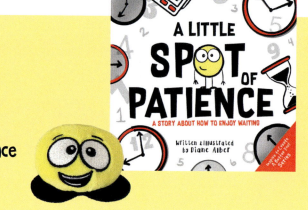

 **Learning Objective:**

Students will learn:
- How to be more polite
- Various situations that require patience
- How to find their calm

 **Reading:**

A Little SPOT of Patience

Introduce the book to the students. Do you know what the word PATIENCE means? This book will help you learn about what it means to be PATIENT!

Reflect on the beginning of the book: There are a lot of situations that require PATIENCE. Some things you may only wait a minute for, and some things you might need to wait years for, like that big apple tree. Can you name some things that you would only need to wait a minute for? Can you think of something that would take years?

Kitchen Scraps Garden-Celery

Materials Needed:

○ Celery   ○ Shallow bowl or dish   ○ Water

Since apple trees are hard to grow, we are going to do a growing experiment with celery!

Step One: Cut off 3" of the bottom of the celery.

Step Two: Place in a shallow dish in 1 inch of water. Replace water after 3 days.

Step Three: Watch your celery grow!

Day 3-shoots   Day 5   Day 8

 Discussion:

How has having patience helped this celery? If you would have taken it out of the water too early, it wouldn't have grown.

 Puppet:

Have the puppet talk about what they do to help themselves stay patient. An example would be, "I look for fun spots around the room!"

 Appendix 171

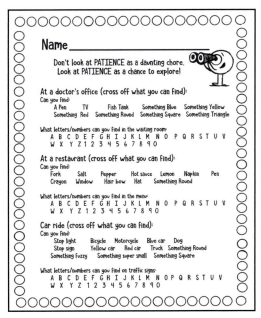

HONESTY

Honesty Is The Best Policy

In order for children to fully succeed in academics, they need to acquire certain skills. Among those skills is honesty. Honesty is more then telling the truth, it's about building trust and having integrity. Children will discover the benefits of being honest and the consequences of being dishonest. It's important to model honesty and provide vivid examples, so students can fully comprehend the concept of honesty.

Learning Objective:
Students will learn:
- The importance of trust
- How to build trust in relationships
- What is honesty

Reading:
A Little SPOT of Honesty
Introduce the book to the students.
Do you know what it means to be honest? This book will help you understand the importance of honesty and trust.

Reflect on the beginning of the book: Did you know being HONEST is MORE than just about telling the TRUTH? It helps you show INTEGRITY and earn RESPECT, too. It also builds strong relationships and encourages people to be HONEST with you.

 Discussion:

Have you ever played a game with someone who didn't follow the rules on purpose? How did that make you feel? Discuss why honesty is important. Ask the questions: What if it was okay to be dishonest? What would happen? Allow the students to talk about what would happen if everyone lied and how they would feel.

Discuss how honesty is important to friendship. Give an example: if every time your friend came over, she took an item from your house without telling you (stealing), how would that make you feel?

Have you ever had someone break their promise to you? Have you ever broken a promise? How did it make you feel?

 Tower Of Trust

Instructions: Build a giant Jenga

Explain to the students that this Jenga represents a tower of trust. When you tell the truth, the tower is strong and untouched. When you tell a lie, it removes a block and becomes wobbly. Over time the weight will increase on top of the tower and become very unsteady. That is what happens when we start breaking trust with people. The relationship becomes weak.

RESPONSIBILITY

Responsibility In The Classroom

The earlier children can learn a sense of responsibility, the better. When children become teenagers, it is usually met with unnecessary resistance. By educating children to be responsible in the classroom, it will also help them be responsible at home. When communicating to children about responsibility, it is very important to make clear intentions and expectations. When addressing behaviors revolving around responsibility, the conversation has to explain what behavior is appropriate and expected. Make sure to use words that are very familiar to children and use more positives than negatives. Focus on the thought process of decision-making and learning to see the consequences of a situation before students make a choice.

Learning Objective:
Students will learn:
- Good decision making
- How to make a good choice

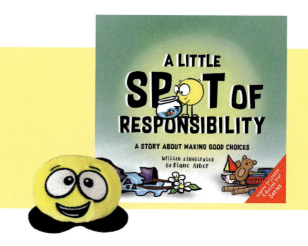

Reading:
A Little SPOT of Responsibility

Introduce the book to the students. Do you know what the word RESPONSIBILITY means? This book will help you learn about what it means to be responsible and make good choices

Reflect back: Every time you make a GOOD CHOICE, your RESPONSIBILITY SPOT GROWS, and it makes you feel more CONFIDENT and HAPPY! Here are a list of common problems. Walk through different ways to make a good choice. Use the example from the book.

Examples of Problems:

You want to keep playing video games, but it's time to eat.

Your parents want you to clean your room, but you don't want to.

Your homework is too hard.

You don't want to come inside from recess.

You want to eat cookies for breakfast.

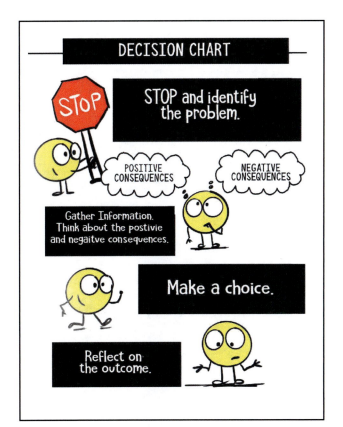

Discussion:

What is a good choice? What is a bad choice?

Can you think of good choices you make every day?

Can you name some good choices you can make in the classroom? (For example, listening, completing your work, waiting your turn, and sharing.)

RESPONSIBILITY

💬 Discussion:

Reflect on the books below. Discuss how Safety, Respect, and Kindness can help you make a good choice.

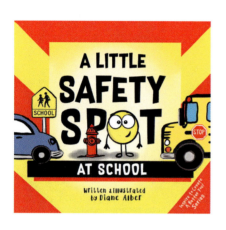
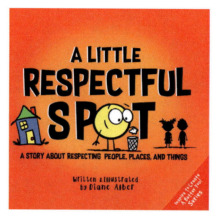
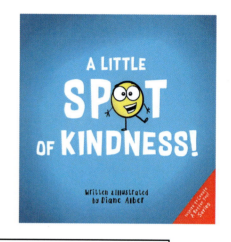

 Appendix 166-167

✋ Desk Chart

A desk chart is a visual representation of a student's progress toward a behavior goal. It can be used as feedback to help students assess their progress in changing problematic behavior and used to help recognize their positive behavior.

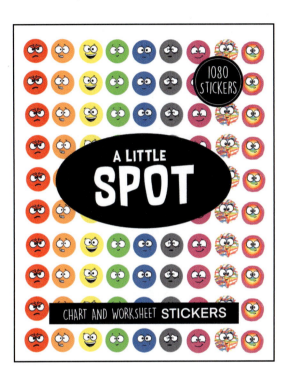

 Appendix 181

💬 Discussion:

Discuss situations at home, in the classroom, and on the playground where students can use their skills to show responsibility.

🗨 Puppet:

Have the puppet talk about what he does to be responsible. For example, "I look for ways to make good choices."

ORGANIZATION

Reduce Frustration And Save Time!

By nature, most children are not organized. While some children may possess organizational skills naturally, most students will need to learn this life skill. If a child can't find their homework, they most likely won't turn it in. If they can't find a writing supply, they will most likely become frustrated, making it harder for them to learn. Organization isn't often taught in school, but these skills need to be learned for success in school.

Learning Objective:
Students will learn:
- The importance of organization
- How to create a schedule

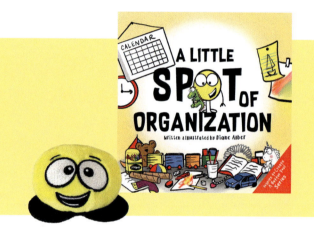

 Reading:

A Little SPOT of Organization

Introduce the book to the students.

Do you know what it means to be organized? This book will show us the benefits of being organized and how organization can help us.

 Reflect on the book: Discuss how the book suggested different ways to be organized. (For example, organizing things, schedules, organizing emotions, organizing a story.) Can you name some things you currently do that are organized?

Visual routine charts can assist students in becoming more independent and less stressed on a daily basis. The benefits of using visual schedules are well-documented, and there are numerous approaches for implementing them. Visual schedules are there to reassure children of exactly what is going to happen. When a child has not learned how to tell time yet, this gives them security in knowing when it is time to eat, play, and sleep. Using a visual schedule in the classroom can show that activites can change, which can help students cope when something unexpected happens. This will also encourage the students to look at the schedule instead of asking when the next activity is.

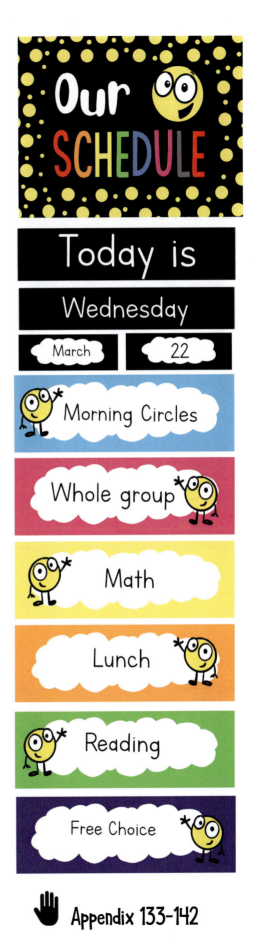

 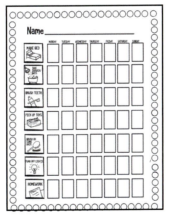

Appendix 161-164

Discussion:

Have you ever lost your favorite toy, or your shoe, or something to complete your assignment? How did that make you feel?

Appendix 133-142

NOTES:

PART THREE: SELF-AWARENESS

- ○ OPTIMISM
- ○ PERSEVERANCE
- ○ TALENT
- ● BOREDOM
- ○ FLEXIBLE THINKING
- ○ COURAGE
- ○ CREATIVITY
- ● FRUSTRATION

SELF-AWARNESS is the ability to comprehend one's own emotions, thoughts, and values. Emotions, thoughts and values influence behavior in different situations. Self-Awareness includes the ability to understand one's own talents and limits while maintaining a strong feeling of self-assurance and purpose.

TEACHING TIPS
- ○ Proactively look for good choices and reinforce them
- ○ Be positive and become a role model for demonstrating SOCIAL SKILLS
- ○ During core subjects, look for opportunities to practice SOCIAL SKILLS

 Reference *Feelings & Emotions Guide*
 Puppet
 Learning Objective
 Educator Reading
 Discussion
 Hands-on: Arts and Crafts
 Hands-on: Worksheets

Reminder: Areas presented in red text are intended to serve as the Educator's script, if needed, for teaching the lesson.

OPTIMISM

Learned Optimism

Learning to be Optimistic involves developing the skills necessary to view the world from a positive point of view. Children that are more optimistic tend to have better mental health, higher motivation, and lower stress. Optimism can also build self-confidence and belief in a child's personal ability.

Learning Objective:

Students will learn:
- How to turn a negative thought into a positive one
- Growth mindset

Reading:

A Little SPOT of Optimism

Introduce the book to the students. Do you know what the word OPTIMISM means? This book will help explain what optimism is and how we can learn to be more optimistic.

Reflect on the beginning of the book:

Yes, there are other phrases that relate to OPTIMISM, like "When life gives you lemons, make LEMONADE." When you apply this to life, it can help you stay POSITIVE even in a SOUR situation. You have the power to make it more enjoyable. Can you think of a sour situation? What if it's raining when you want to go and play? What could you do to make things better (lemonade?)

✋ Lemonade In A Bag!

Materials Needed:

- ⬤ Lemon Wedge ⬤ Sugar
- ⬤ Ice ⬤ Ziplock bag ⬤ Straw
- ⬤ Water

Step One: Hand out a lemon wedge, straw, and Ziplock bag to every student. Have them squeeze the lemon in the bag and have them take a small drink with the straw.

Is that super sour? Sometimes when life gives you sour lemons, you have to find a way to make sweet lemonade!

Step Two: Now go around and give the kids a 1/4 cup of water, ice, and a teaspoon of sugar. Have them mix it up again.

✋ Appendix 155

OPTIMISM

 # Push Out Negative Thoughts

Materials Needed:
- Toilet Paper Roll
- Cotton Ball
- Marker

Before the lesson color half of the cotton balls with a black or gray marker.

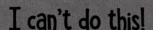 NEGATIVE THOUGHTS

POSITIVE THOUGHTS

NEGATIVE THOUGHTS	POSITIVE THOUGHTS
I can't do this!	I can't do this YET! I just need to practice.
I made a mistake.	Mistakes help me learn.
This is too hard.	It's just going to take some time and effort to figure it out.

Sometimes when a negative thought enters your mind, it can be difficult to change it into a positive thought. I want to show you a visual of how positive thoughts can actually push negative thoughts out of your mind!

Instructions:

Load some negative thoughts (gray color cotton balls) into the tube. Now every time you put some more cotton balls in the tube say a positive thought, and watch how the negative thoughts pour out. Can you think of more positive thoughts? Every time you give me another positive thought, I will add another cotton ball.

I can't do this, YET!
I just need to practice.

I can't do this!

Appendix 156-157

PERSEVERANCE

Failure And Learning

It is critical to teach children the value of perseverance because it motivates them to pursue their goals and overcome obstacles. Without perseverance, children would never learn to walk, climb, or run. Young children will often try and fail, revise and try again to grow and learn. Unfortunately, it's often adult and peer reactions to failure that influences a child to interpret failure as a bad thing instead of associating failure with learning and growth.

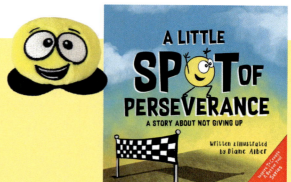

 Learning Objective:

Students will learn:
- What to do when they make a mistake
- How failure leads to learning

 **Reading:**

A Little SPOT of Perseverance

Introduce the book to the students. Do you know what PERSEVERANCE means? This book will show us what to do when we feel like giving up.

 **Discussion:**

Have you ever felt like giving up? Have you ever kept going even though what you were doing was hard? How did it make you feel?

🎨 Continued Drawing

Imagine what would happen if some of the most famous artists quit after they produced just one line? They would never get to see all their amazing masterpieces and learn from their mistakes. We are going to help finish these drawings, so they can become something great!

Have the students complete the scribble and write a story!

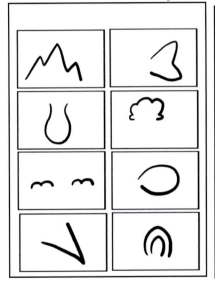 

✋ Appendix 189-193

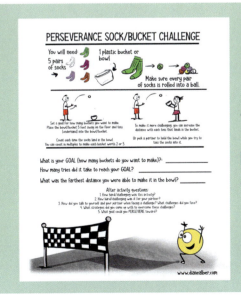

✋ Sock Throw

This fun activity will test students' skill and also provide a real-life challenge that will allow them to practice perseverance.

Appendix 150

PERSEVERANCE

 ## Carrot, Egg or Cocoa

Materials Needed:

- Carrot
- Egg
- Cocoa
- Pot to boil water
- Mug

Show the class the three items: a carrot, egg, and cocoa. What do you see? A Carrot, Egg, and Hot Cocoa. I'm going to place each item in its own pot of boiling water. What do you think will happen? If you don't have access to a pot of boiling water at school, you can preboil all the items at home and bring them to class.

The boiling water represents a challenge or difficult experience, and each of these items will react differently.

 ## Discussion:

Can you think of a challenge in your life? Or a difficult experience?

Now ask the class to feel the carrot that was boiled.
The carrot went in strong but came out mushy.

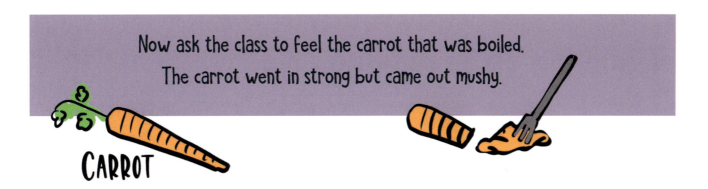

Ask the student to break the hard-boiled egg.
The egg went in fragile but came out with a hardened center.

Now ask the class to smell the hot cocoa. The cocoa is unique. It's no longer just a dull powder but now has a wonderful smell.

Are you Carrot, Egg, or Cocoa?

We all have a choice when faced with a challenge. We can be like the carrot and lose strength. We can become the egg that starts off with a soft heart but becomes hardened. Or we can become the hot cocoa and embrace what was put in the way to challenge us. In the example with the cocoa, it actually got better with change! You can have a hot cocoa party after the lesson!

COURAGE

Courage In Everyday Life

Courage shows up when fear is present. Because children are still learning the difference between fear that is meant to keep them safe and fear that motivates them to make good choices, we must be good role models and praise students when they demonstrate courage. We must also recognize times when they struggle to make a good choice and use that time as a learning opportunity. Even the simple act of asking for help can take courage.

Learning Objective:

Students will learn:
- What it means to have courage
- Things they can do to help build a courage SPOT

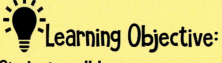 Reading:

A Little SPOT of Courage

Introduce the book to the students.

Do you know what the word COURAGE means? This book will help show you ways you can show courage even if you are scared or afraid.

 **Reflect on the beginning of the book:** I'm here to help you do something that is challenging or difficult, especially when you are afraid.

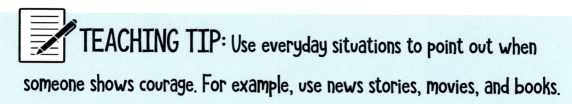

TEACHING TIP: Use everyday situations to point out when someone shows courage. For example, use news stories, movies, and books.

💬 **Discussion:** Can you think of everyday situations when you are afraid or scared to do something that you know is good for you or someone else?
Stand up when someone isn't being treated good. Refuse to go along with the crowd when the crowd is doing something wrong or dangerous. What about the first day of school at a new school or admitting you did something wrong even though you might get in trouble?

Complimentry books for this lesson as well.:

📖 **Reflect on the book:** You don't need to wear a cape to have COURAGE. COURAGE is inside all of us, and we can do small or large acts of COURAGE every day.

✋ ## Courage Cards

After you have read the book, show the class the courage cards and explain how you will be giving courage cards when you see someone's courage spot growing. Reflect on all the different cards in the book.

Appendix 174

For extended lessons on ANXIETY, WORRY, and CONFIDENCE reference *Feelings & Emotions Guide* 56-61, 70-72

TALENT

Finding Your Way To Shine!

Talent is the natural ability to do something well, especially without being taught. Every child has talents that can be promoted. You need to help childrens' talents emerge by creating the right environment. Talents and strengths usually go hand in hand. To embrace and grow their talent, children need stregth like courage, perservance, self-control, and empathy.

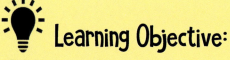

Learning Objective:

Students will learn:
- How to discover their strengths
- How to find their talent

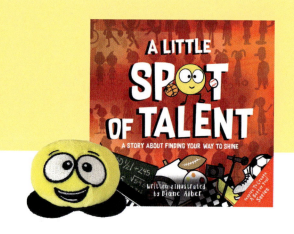

A Little SPOT of Talent

Introduce the book to the students. Do you know what Talent is? This book will help you learn all about talents and how each and every one of us has a talent that can be shared with the world even if we might not have discovered it yet.

There may be talents that you don't know even exist, like talking backward, eyebrow dancing, walking like a crab, singing with your mouth closed, even pen spinning (Yes! There is a YouTube video on kids spinning pens. Search "Extreme Pen Spinning.")

 Discussion:

Discuss some different talents. For example: mathematician, pianist, ping pong player, artist, musician, gamer, etc.

Print out the map below, and bring out all the books that are on this map to show the class. Discuss how each of the skills on this map helps us find our talent!

 Appendix 173

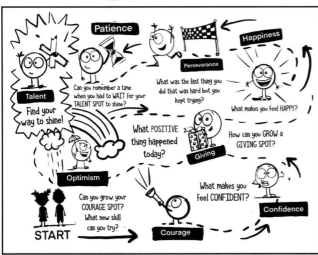

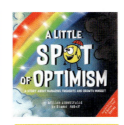
Having a POSITIVE outlook helps you look at things differently. When you can shift your MINDSET, it is easier to keep working in challenging situations.

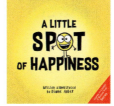
Think about what makes you happy. What do you like talking about? Can you do an activity for hours like drawing or painting!

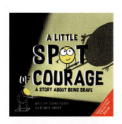
You need COURAGE to try as many new skills as you can, even if you are scared or embarrassed, so you can find your TALENTS.

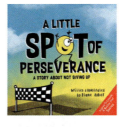
You can PERSEVERE and keep trying when things become hard or challenging.

Did you know when you are TALENTED at something, it can make you feel CONFIDENT, too? Make a list of all the things that you feel CONFIDENT doing.

If you still haven't found your TALENT SPOT, that's okay! It can take some time to find out what you're good at!

When you GIVE your time to help others, you not only have an opportunity to experience new things, but you also can meet new people!

BOREDOM, in the next chapter, is a great way to find your TALENT too!

TALENT

My Talents

Materials Needed:
- Student picture
- Abstract Art
- Scissors
- Glue
- Camera

Instructions:

Step One: Take a picture with a white background.

Step Two: Print it in black and white and cut it out.

Step Three: Glue it onto a piece of abstract art.

Appendix 149

Talent Mobile

Materials Needed:
- Paper Circles 2"
- White Yarn
- Glue
- 1 Embroidery ring

Instructions:

Cut out ovals or circles in different color construction papers. Each student will receive two. On one circle, they will draw a self-portrait, and on the other circle they will write a word that will help them find their talent.

Examples would be:

Tie the yarn to the embroidery ring and paste the two sides together from the hanging string.

CREATIVITY

Self-Expression

Creativity is the most liberating mode of self-expression. Nothing is more rewarding and fulfilling for children than being able to express themselves freely and without fear. However, teaching creativity to children who are under pressure from adults can be difficult. The best way to inspire creativity in your students is for them to learn how to use their imaginations, to think for themselves, and to discover new things and applications for things they already know.

 Learning Objective:

Students will learn:
- ○ Self-expression
- ○ How to "think outside of the box"

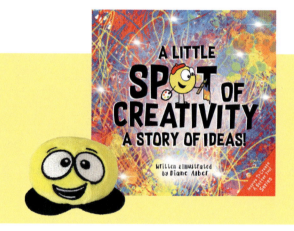

 Reading:

A Little SPOT of Creativity

Introduce the book to the students. Ask if they know what the word CREATIVITY means. This book will show you what it means to be creative and even inspire some creativity, too!

Reflect on the beginning of the book: MUSIC is another way to inspire CREATIVITY! Music can actually help your brain learn and perform better! It can help change your mood, too! What's your favorite song? How does that song make you feel?

✋ Creative Brain Break

I'm going to show you how you can turn pretty much anything into a musical instrument with just with a little imagination! All you need is pool noodles from the dollar store and cut them in half, or in thirds. You can use the desk or a chair.

Great music to play:
"We Will Rock You" by Queen
"Believer" by Imagine Dragons
You can search YouTube for cardio desk drumming to get a video tutorial! Alright, here were go. Drumroll! Tap, tap.....tap, tap, tap....stomp stomp!

BOREDOM

Boredom Is Good For You!

Students can be bored in the classroom for a variety of reasons, but it usually comes from either a lack of challenge or a lack of interest in the subject matter being covered. After studying boredom, I discovered there are actually two different types of BOREDOM. Understanding how each one works can actually make Boredom a good thing!

Learning Objective:

Students will learn:
- The different kinds of BOREDOM
- How to spark creativity

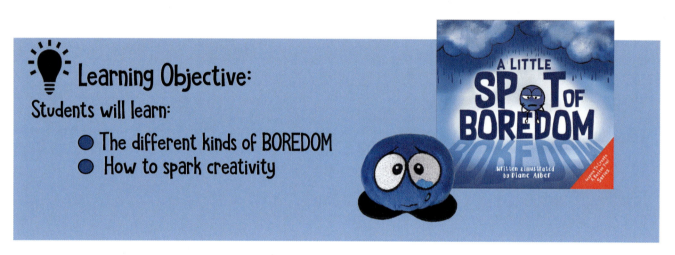

Reading:

A Little SPOT of Boredom

Introduce the book to the students. Who knows what the word BOREDOM means? This book will help you understand why we feel BOREDOM and what we can do!

Reflect on the beginning of the book: There are actually two different types of BOREDOM: NO TASK BOREDOM and TASK BOREDOM. It's important to know the difference because they each show up at different times. Can you think of situations that you had NO TASK Boredom? Like maybe you couldn't think of anything to do on the weekend? Or TASK BOREDOM, like when you didn't want to do your homework?

 Discussion:

Have the students brainstorm times that they experienced either kinds of BOREDOMS, and ask how they felt. What did they do during that time to spark their boredom into creativity?

BOREDOM Bubble Painting:

Materials needed: ● Nontoxic tempera ● Paint ● Dish soap ● Cups or small bowls ● Construction paper or card stock ● Tablespoon ● Straw

Step One: Add about 2 tablespoons of paint (good amount), 1 tablespoon of dish soap, and 3 tablespoons of water to each cup.

Step Two: Mix each cup using the straw and start blowing bubbles in the cup. Once the bubbles rise above the rim of the cup, scoop bubbles onto the paper. Then pop the bubbles with your finger and repeat with different color paint. It's as simple as that!

Scoop the bubbles!

FLEXIBLE THINKING

Think Like A PALM TREE!

Some children have difficulty switching gears. They can become nervous or frustrated when their schedule is disrupted. When confronted with a dilemma, children who have trouble with flexible thinking may freeze and do nothing, or they might keep trying the same method, even if it doesn't work. Helping children develop a growth mindset and the ability to problem-solve will help them through their entire lives.

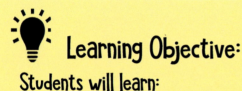

Learning Objective:

Students will learn:
- How to problem-solve
- How to remain calm in a frustrating situation
- How to have a growth mindset

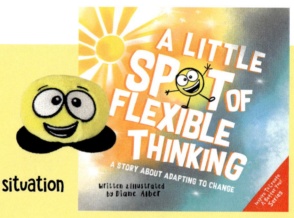

Reading:

A Little SPOT of Flexible Thinking

Introduce the book to the students.

This book will help you learn about what it means how to work as a team!

Discussion:

Have you ever become frustrated when something didn't work out the way you wanted to?

Have you ever expected something to happen, and it didn't? How did you feel? What did you do?

RIGID OAK TREES are STRONG with deep, thick roots!

Their trunk and branches are NOT very BENDABLE. They can SNAP in half with a strong wind.

FLEXIBLE PALM TREES have very thin, spaghetti-like roots.

Their bodies are BENDABLE and ADAPTABLE. They can easily move with the wind. They can BEND UP TO 50 degrees without BREAKING! That's almost half their body!

Paper vs. Popsicle Stick

 Appendix 183

Materials Needed:
- ○ Paper cut into a strip
- ○ Popsicle stick
- ○ Change worksheet

Show the class a strip of paper and a popsicle stick. These items are both made of trees, but they react to bending differently. Try to bend the popsicle stick. This popsicle stick is like the oak tree; it's rigid and does not bend easily. Now show the class the strip of paper and show how easily it can bend. When the oak tree needed to bend with the wind, it didn't and snapped, but the palm tree flowed with wind. Sometimes when change happens, being flexible will prevent you from getting frustrated and disappointed.

Students can create the PALM TREE and OAK TREE characters in the book and see how flexible they are!

Step One: Print out the Change worksheet and decorate it.
Step Two: Create a Palm TREE using a strip of paper and some paper leaves.
Step Three: Create an Oak TREE using a popsicle stick and paper leaves.
Step Four: Tape both trees to the Change worksheet using one strip of tape on the bottom of the trunks. Now you can see how each of them bends with CHANGE!

FRUSTRATION

Cranky Students

Frustration might be your students' biggest hurdle in accomplishing their objectives. Children become frustrated frequently at school when they are challenged to learn something new or when they are interacting with their peers. Although both situations happen very often, it's important to help your students understand these feelings and learn how to process them in a healthy way.

Learning Objective:

Students will learn:
- How to control emotions
- How mistakes lead to growth
- How to reflect on choices to improve future choices

Reading:

A Little SPOT of Frustration

Introduce the book to the students. Do you know what the word FRUSTRATION means? This book will help show you how to be flexible in tough situations.

Reflect on the beginning of the book: FRUSTRATION SPOTS get confused easily. Little problems, like misplacing your pencil, can TRIGGER a FRUSTRATION SPOT when all that is needed was a FLEXIBLE THINKING SPOT. How do we know what size a problem is? Can you name some small problems?

Can you name some big problems?

 Frustration Token

 Discussion:

Discuss situations at home, in the classroom, or on the playground when students have been frustrated.

What are some tools you have used to help bring yourself back to your PEACEFUL SPOT?

1. COLOR AND CUT OUT EACH SIDE OF THE TOKEN.
2. GLUE OR TAPE THE BLANK SIDES TOGETHER.
3. NOW PRACTICE FLIPPING THE TOKEN BY TURNING IT OVER AND OVER AGAIN!

 Appendix 159

Complimentry books for this lesson as well:

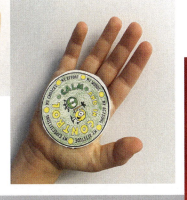
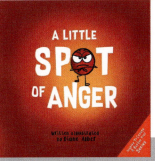

 For extended lessons CALM and ANGER reference *Feelings & Emotions Guide* page 44-49, 52-55

Reflect on this part of the book: Why do I keep making mistakes?

💬 Discussion:

Model for the class by sharing an example from your own life when you made a mistake, but it helped you learn. (For example, when you accidentally left a box of crayons in the hot car, and they all melted together. You were upset that you ruined your crayons but realized that it could make a cool blended color.) Ask the students to share a mistake they made and how it helped them grow. What do mistakes show us? Were you able to improve after your mistake?

Puppet:

Use the puppet to talk about specific situations where someone could make a mistake.

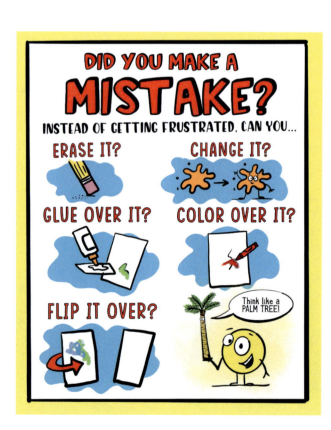

Appendix 185-186

Reflect on this part of the book: Being able to reflect and remember when you were able to FLIP a FRUSTRATION SPOT to a CALM SPOT can help you with future FRUSTRATION SPOTS! Reflecting on what happened and what choice you made, and what choice you shouldn't have made is a great way to learn from your frustrations!

 Appendix 182

 **Discussion:**

Sometimes we get frustrated and take it out on other people. It's important for us to recognize how our frustrations can actually make others feel upset. Can you think of a time when you yelled at someone when you were frustrated? How did that make them feel? How have you CALMED yourself down?

 For extended lessons on finding your PEACEFUL SPOT reference *Feelings & Emotions Guide* page 44-51

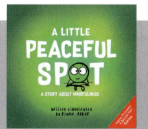

NOTES:

APPENDIX: ACTIVITY RESOURCES

This guide refers to multiple printouts for you to use with the lessons. Make copies (30 print limit) and use them with the students.

 TEACHING REMINDER

○ Get creative.
○ Try to give each student a few minutes of undivided attention.
○ There are valuable lessons that students can learn when working with groups. Use these opportunities to teach FEELINGS and how to respect the FEELINGS of others.

Get to know you BINGO

SIT or STAND
What do you have in common?

SIT   **STAND**

 Would you rather have a dog or cat?

 Would you rather play soccer or baseball?

 Would you rather draw or paint?

 Would you rather sing or dance?

 Would you rather have a pet unicorn or dinosaur?

 Would you rather have an apple or banana?

 Would rather live in the ocean or in space?

TEAM BUTTER

MATERIALS NEEDED:

HEAVY WHIPPING CREAM + MASON JAR OR BABY FOOD JAR + SALT (OPTIONAL) +

DIRECTIONS:

THE JAR NEEDS TO BE SHAKEN FOR AT LEAST 15 MINUTES. IF YOU HAVE 20 STUDENTS, EACH STUDENT WILL NEED TO SHAKE THE JAR FOR 45 SECONDS.

STEP 1: FILL THE JAR HALF WAY WITH CREAM

STEP 2: HAVE CHILDREN SHAKE AND PASS THE JAR UNTIL THE CREAM SEPARATES INTO A LUMP OF BUTTER AND BUTTERMILK

STEP 3: HAVE THE EDUCATOR REMOVE THE BUTTER AND RINSE OFF BUTTERMILK UNDER COLD WATER OR SHAKE WITH AN ICE CUBE

STEP 4: (OPTIONAL) STIR IN A TOUCH OF SALT AND SPREAD ON CRACKERS FOR THE CLASS

Name: _____

TEAM BUTTER

MATERIALS NEEDED:

HEAVY WHIPPING CREAM + MASON JAR + SALT + CRACKER

How many team members? _____

Who is the leader? _____

How long does each teammate shake the glass? _____

Our cream went from a _____

To a _____

DRAW BEFORE AND AFTER

BEFORE   AFTER

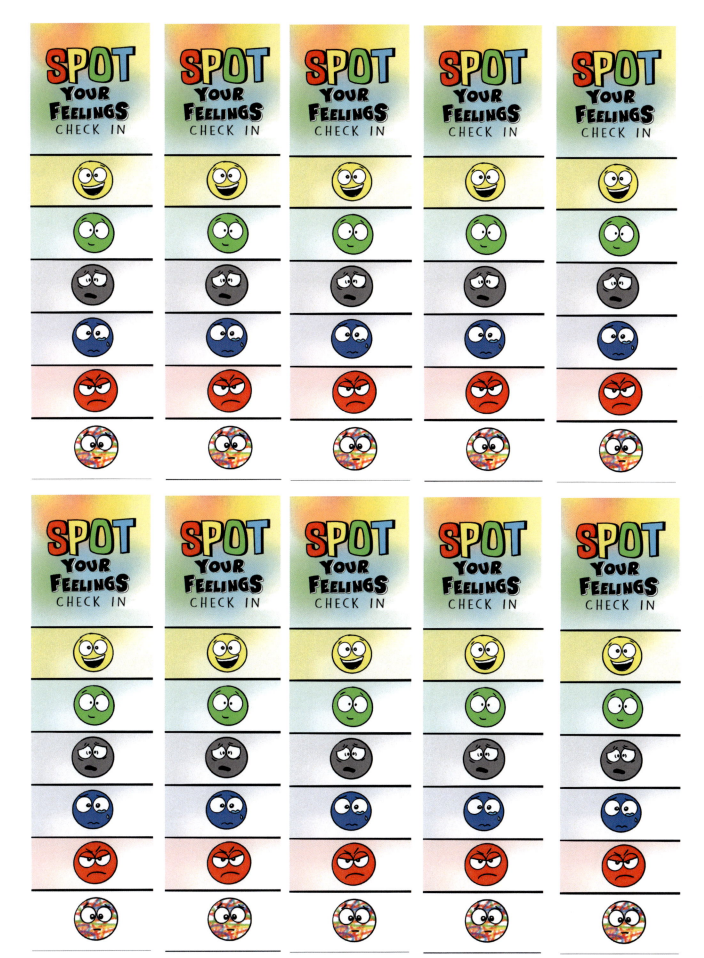

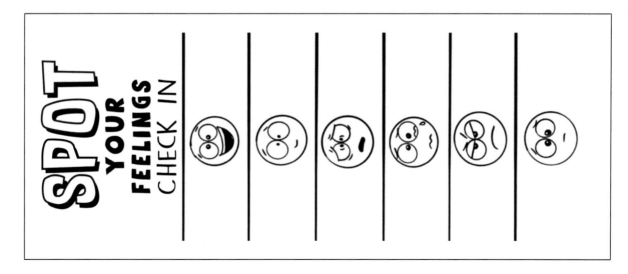

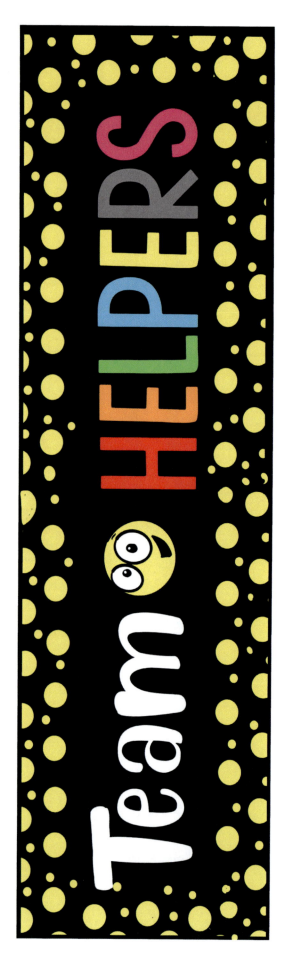
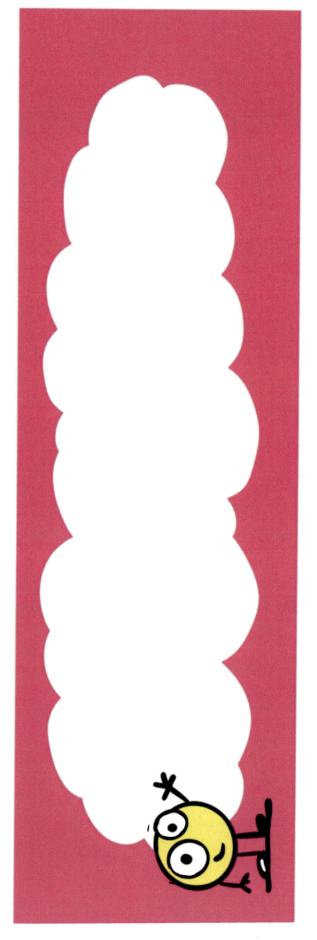

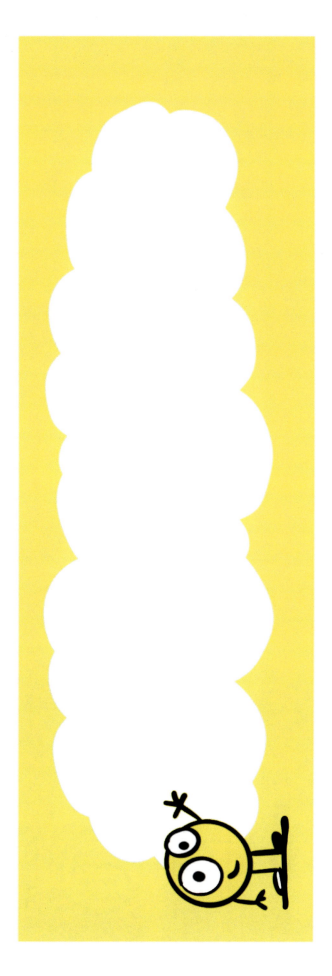

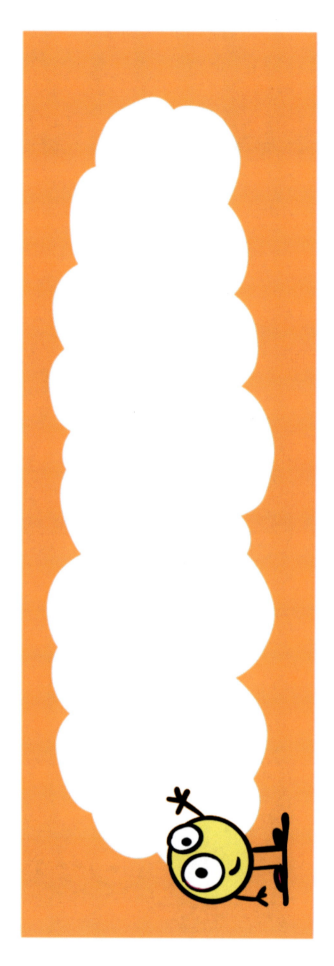
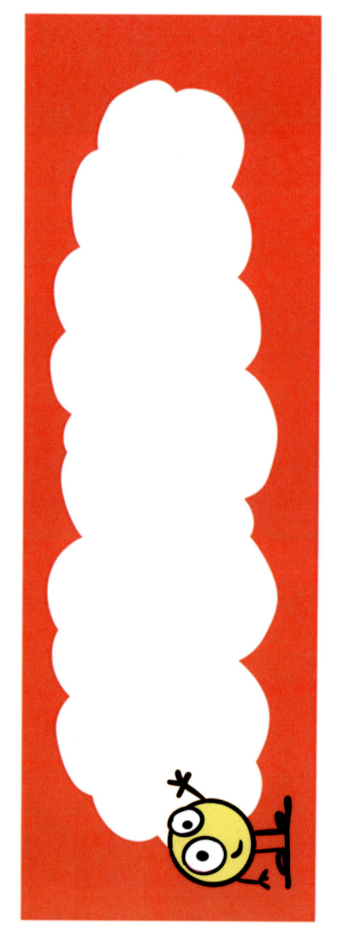

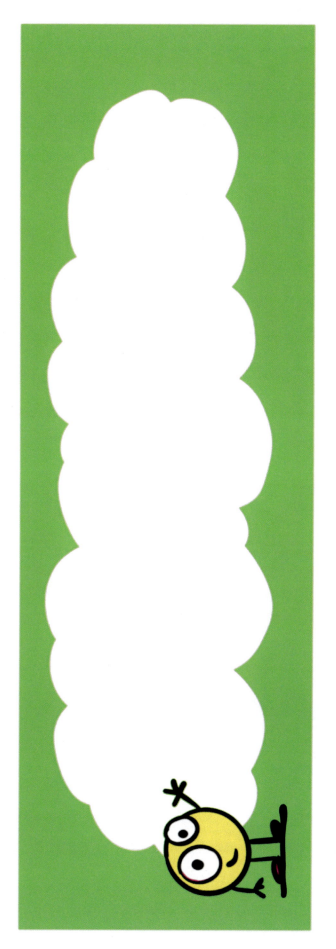

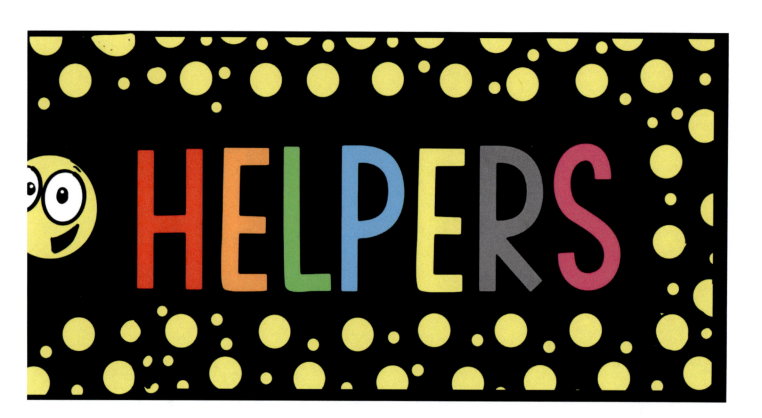

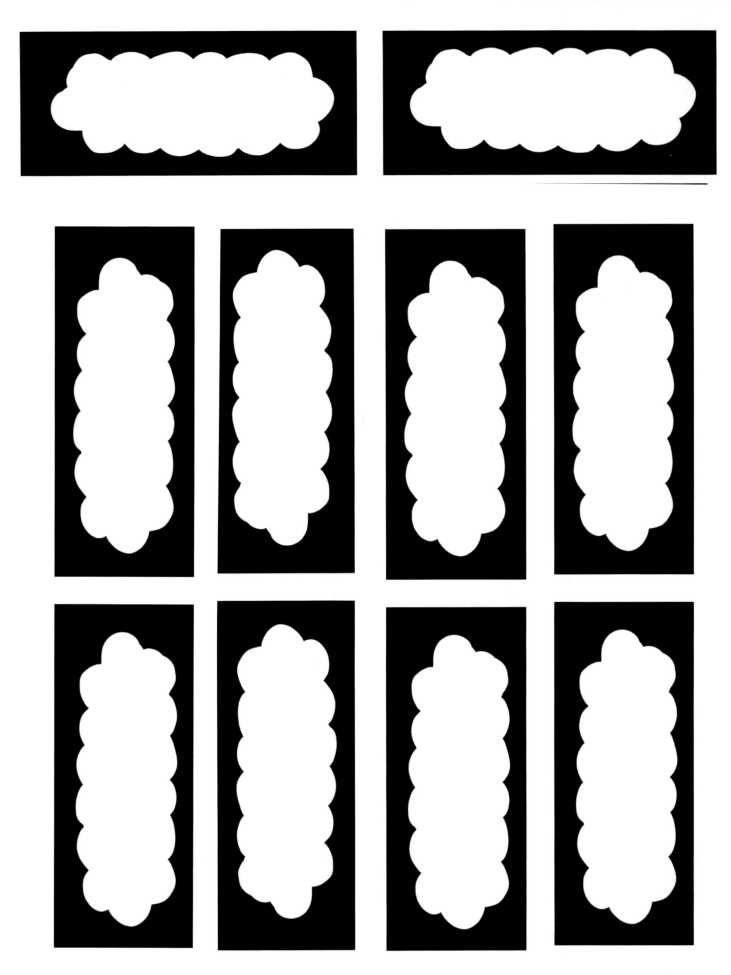

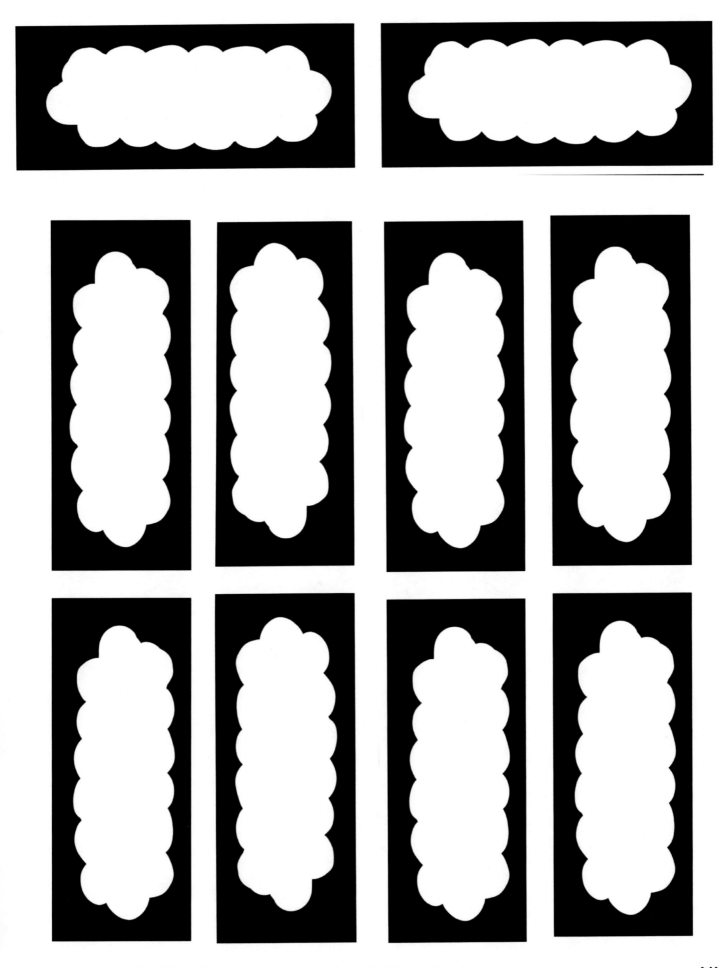

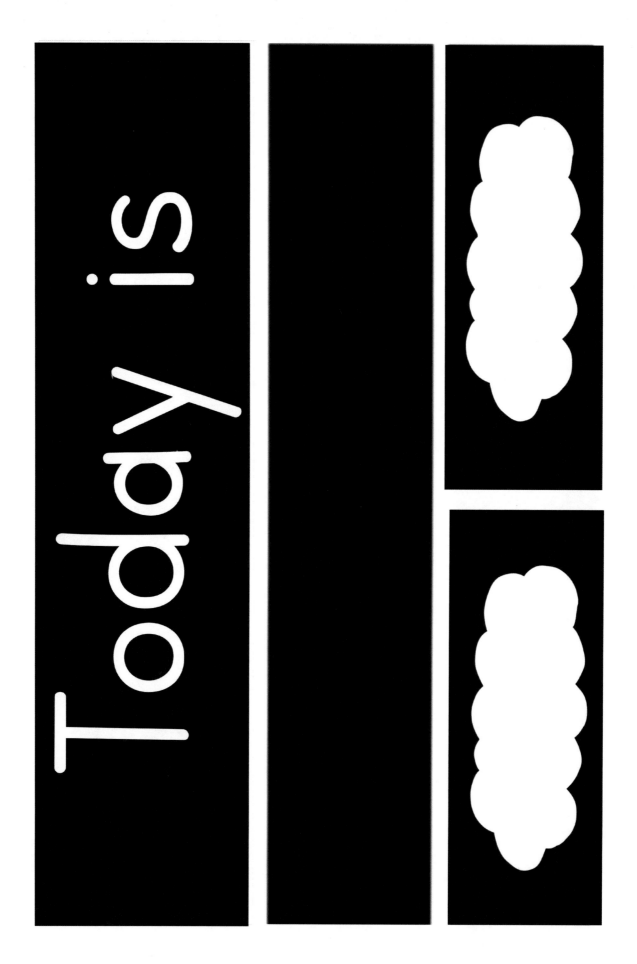

Name: _____

KANDINSKY APPLE

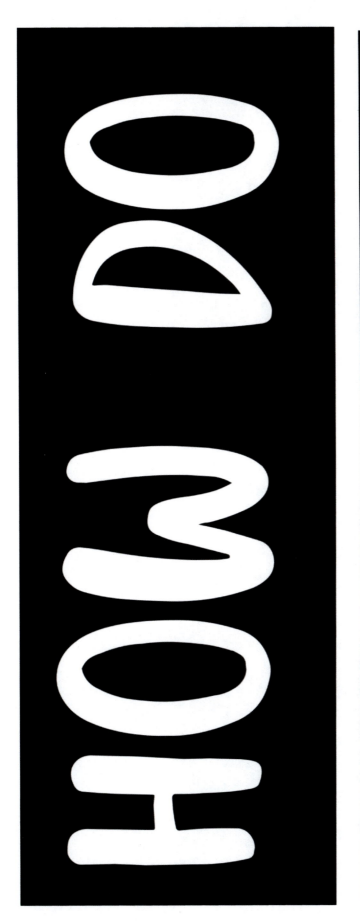
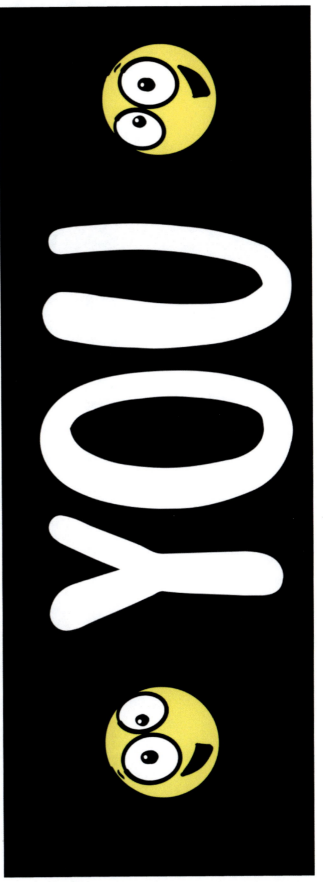

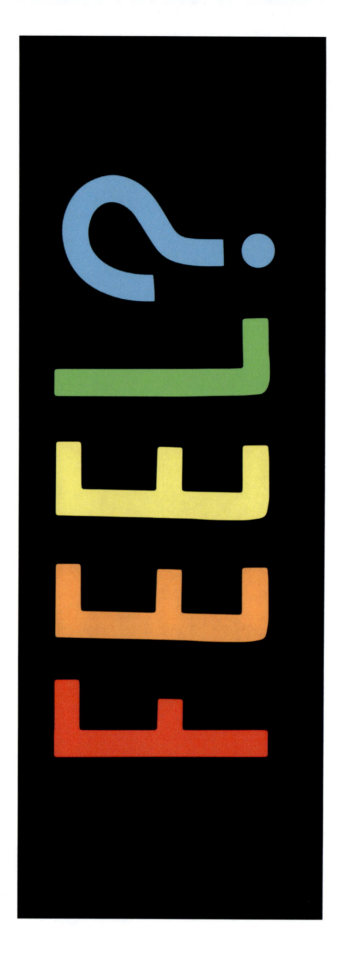

PERSEVERANCE SOCK/BUCKET CHALLENGE

You will need: 5 pairs of socks, 1 plastic bucket or bowl

Make sure every pair of socks is rolled into a ball.

Set a goal for how many buckets you want to make. Place the bowl/bucket 5 feet away on the floor and toss (underhand) into the bowl/bucket.

Count each time the socks land in the bowl. You can count in multiples to make each basket worth 2 or 5.

To make it more challenging, you can increase the distance with each toss that lands in the bucket.

Or pick a partner to hold the bowl while you try to toss the socks into it.

What is your GOAL (how many buckets do you want to make)?: _____

How many tries did it take to reach your GOAL? _____

What was the farthest distance you were able to make it in the bowl? _____

After activity questions:
1. How hard/challenging was this activity?
2. How hard/challenging was it for your partner?
3. How did you talk to yourself and your partner when facing a challenge? What challenges did you face?
4. What strategies did you come up with to overcome these challenges?
5. What goal could you PERSEVERE toward?

www.dianealber.com

FIND THE EMOTION

Find and circle the emotion words.
Words can run from left to right, right to left, or up and down.

```
S W P M R I S Q F Y
A H A P P I N E S S
D P E A C E F U L A
N O A I E Q S S N N
E H Q K W R A M C G
S S C R I B B L E E
S T A N X I E T Y R
C O N F I D E N C E
X P G O T J D W Q C
H X G W B E L O V E
```

CONFIDENCE

HAPPINESS

PEACEFUL

SADNESS

SCRIBBLE

ANGER

ANXIETY

LOVE

FIND THE EMOTION

FIND AND CIRCLE THE EMOTION WORDS.
WORDS CAN RUN FROM LEFT TO RIGHT, RIGHT TO LEFT, OR UP AND DOWN.

```
S W P M R I S O F Y
A H A P P I N E S S
D P E A C E F U L A
N O A I E Q S S N N
E H Q K W R A M C G
S S C R I B B L E E
S T A N X I E T Y R
  C O N F I D E N C E
X P G O T J D W Q C
H X G W B E L O V E
```

CONFIDENCE   HAPPINESS   PEACEFUL   SADNESS

SCRIBBLE   ANGER   ANXIETY   LOVE

Name: _____

WHO IS WHO

HOW MANY SPOT BOOKS HAVE YOU READ? TRY AND MATCH THE EMOTION WITH THE DESCRIPTION

1. ☐ WHEN YOU FEEL WORRIED OR SCARED

2. ☐ WHEN YOU FEEL CALM AND RELAXED

3. ☐ WHEN YOU FEEL FRUSTRATED

4. ☐ WHEN YOU BELIEVE IN YOURSELF

5. ☐ WHEN YOU FEEL VALUED AND SPECIAL

6. ☐ WHEN YOU FEEL UPSET OR LOST

7. ☐ WHEN YOU FEEL JOY

8. ☐ WHEN YOUR EMOTIONS ARE TANGLED

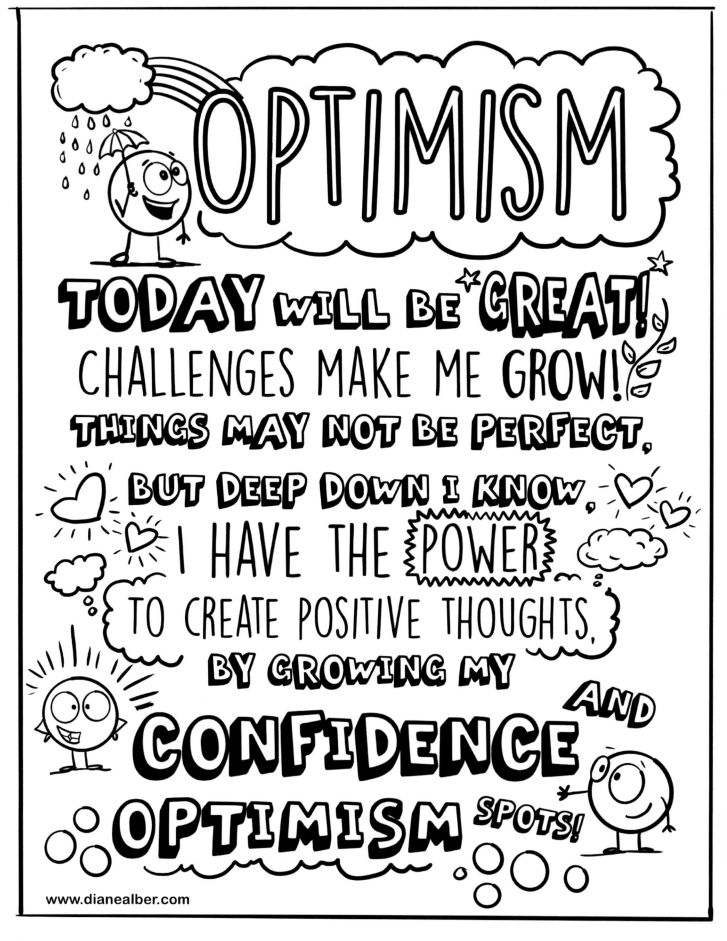

FRUSTRATION FLIP TOKEN

1. COLOR AND CUT OUT EACH SIDE OF THE TOKEN.
2. GLUE OR TAPE THE BLANK SIDES TOGETHER.
3. NOW PRACTICE FLIPPING THE TOKEN BY TURNING IT OVER AND OVER AGAIN!

DECISION CHART

STOP and identify the problem.

POSITIVE CONSEQUENCES

NEGATIVE CONSEQUENCES

Gather Information. Think about the postivie and negaitve consequences.

Make a choice.

Reflect on the outcome.

HOME DAILY SCHEDULE

Name _____

	MONDAY	TUESDAY	WEDNESDAY	THURSDAY	FRIDAY	SATURDAY	SUNDAY
MAKE BED 							
 TAKE SHOWER/BATH							
BRUSH TEETH 							
PICK UP TOYS 							
BRUSH OR COMB HAIR 							
TURN OFF LIGHTS 							
HOMEWORK 							

HOME DAILY SCHEDULE

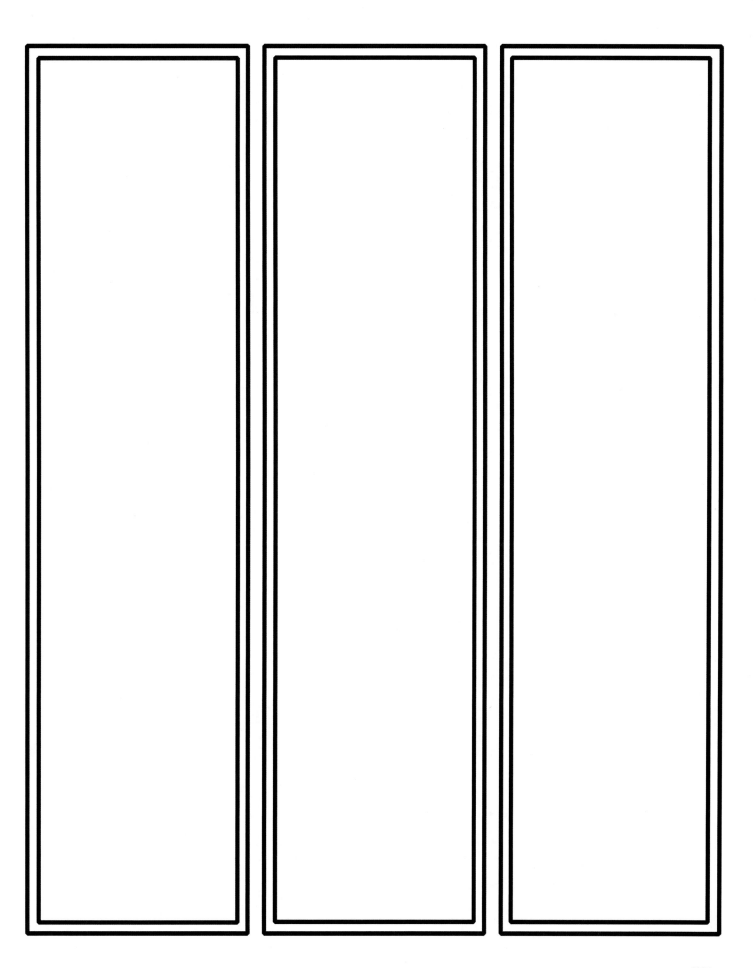

How to Make a Good Choice?

ASK YOURSELF:

Is it Safe?

Is it Respectful?

PEOPLE   PLACES   THINGS

Is it Kind?

How to Make a Good Choice?

ASK YOURSELF:

Is it Safe?

Is it Respectful?

PEOPLE   PLACES   THINGS

Is it Kind?

PERSONAL SAFETY INFORMATION

My full name is: _____

My age is: _____

My siblings names are: _____

My address is:
_____
_____

My emergency contact person's number is:
☐☐☐ - ☐☐☐ - ☐☐☐☐

PERSONAL SAFETY INFORMATION

My full name is: _____

My age is: _____

My siblings names are: _____

My address is:
_____
_____

My emergency contact person's number is:
☐☐☐ - ☐☐☐ - ☐☐☐☐

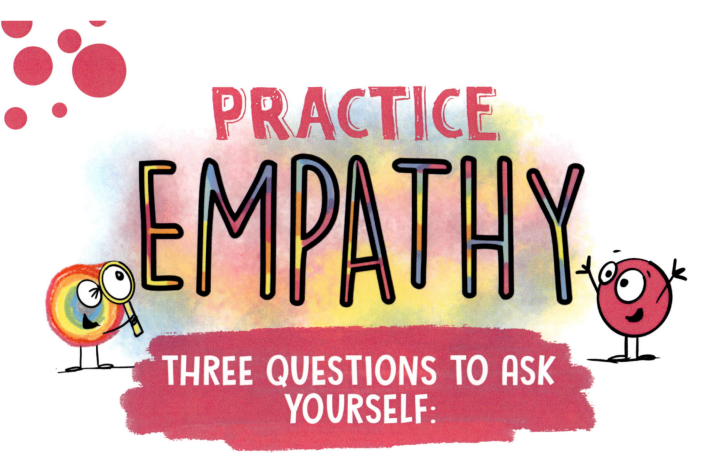

PRACTICE EMPATHY

THREE QUESTIONS TO ASK YOURSELF:

1. WHAT COULD THE PERSON BE FEELING?

2. HAVE I FELT THAT WAY BEFORE?

3. HOW WOULD I WANT TO BE TREATED?

A LITTLE SPOT OF EMPATHY

PRACTICE EMPATHY

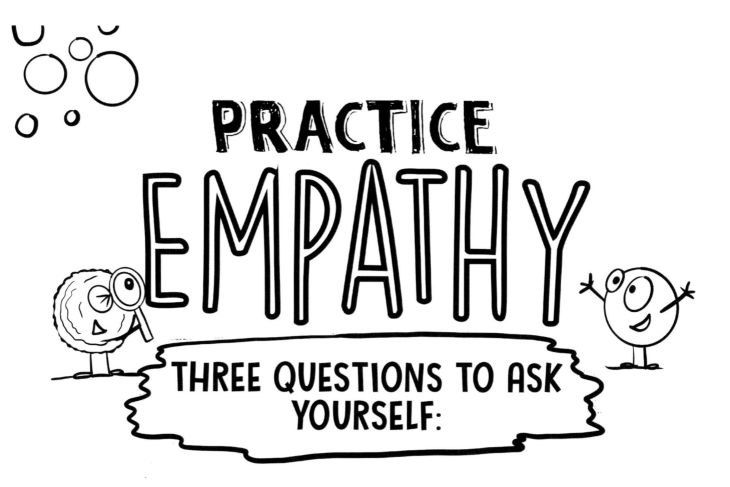

THREE QUESTIONS TO ASK YOURSELF:

1. WHAT COULD THE PERSON BE FEELING?

2. HAVE I FELT THAT WAY BEFORE?

3. HOW WOULD I WANT TO BE TREATED?

A LITTLE SPOT OF EMPATHY

Name_____

Don't look at PATIENCE as a daunting chore.
Look at PATIENCE as a chance to explore!

At a doctor's office (cross off what you can find):
Can you find:
- A Pen
- TV
- Fish Tank
- Something Blue
- Something Yellow
- Something Red
- Something Round
- Something Square
- Something Triangle

What letters/numbers can you find in the waiting room:
A B C D E F G H I J K L M N O P Q R S T U V
W X Y Z 1 2 3 4 5 6 7 8 9 0

At a restaurant (cross off what you can find):
Can you find:
- Fork
- Salt
- Pepper
- Hot sauce
- Lemon
- Napkin
- Pen
- Crayon
- Window
- Hair bow
- Hat
- Something Round

What letters/numbers can you find in the menu:
A B C D E F G H I J K L M N O P Q R S T U V
W X Y Z 1 2 3 4 5 6 7 8 9 0

Car ride (cross off what you can find):
Can you find:
- Stop light
- Bicycle
- Motorcycle
- Blue car
- Dog
- Stop sign
- Yellow car
- Red car
- Truck
- Something Round
- Something fuzzy
- Something super small
- Something Square

What letters/numbers can you find on traffic signs:
A B C D E F G H I J K L M N O P Q R S T U V
W X Y Z 1 2 3 4 5 6 7 8 9 0

Name _____

1. What are you THANKFUL for that is RED?
_____

2. What are you THANKFUL for that makes you smile?
_____

3. What are you THANKFUL for that is soft?
_____

4. What are you THANKFUL for that is very BIG?
_____

5. What are you THANKFUL for that is very small?
_____

6. What person are you THANKFUL for?
_____

7. What animal are you THANKFUL for?
_____

8. What toy are you THANKFUL for?
_____

9. What do you think dogs are THANKFUL for?
_____

10. What book are you THANKFUL for?
_____

○ COURAGE CARD	○ COURAGE CARD
○ COURAGE CARD	○ COURAGE CARD
○ COURAGE CARD	○ COURAGE CARD
○ COURAGE CARD	○ COURAGE CARD

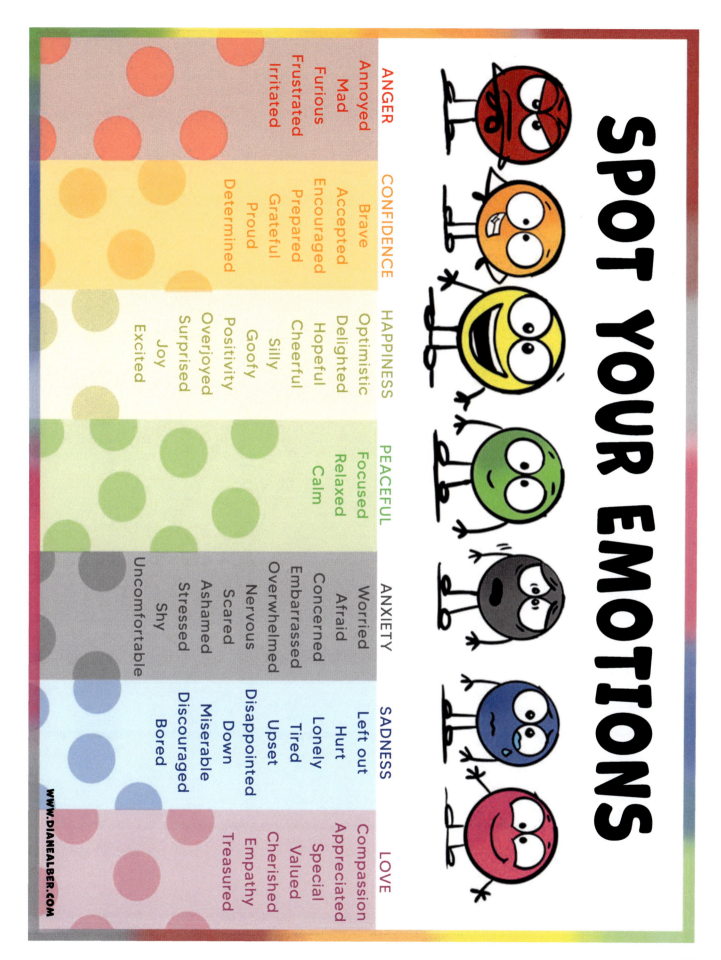

Name _____

What GIFT will you GIVE today?
Who will you GIVE it to?

_____
_____
_____

Name _____

How would you GIVE these GIFTS?

FRIENDSHIP
_____
_____
_____

TEAMWORK
_____
_____
_____

HELPING
_____
_____
_____

SHARING
_____
_____
_____

 # CALM YOUR WORRY

SPOT CHART

NAME _____

IF YOU CAN CALM DOWN YOUR WORRY SPOT...
PLACE A STICKER IN AN EMPTY DOT!

◯ ◯ ◯ ◯ ◯

◯ ◯ ◯ ◯ ◯

REWARD

 # CALM YOUR ANGER

SPOT CHART

NAME _____

IF YOU CAN CALM DOWN YOUR ANGRY SPOT...
PLACE A STICKER IN AN EMPTY DOT!

○ ○ ○ ○ ○

○ ○ ○ ○ ○

REWARD

NAME

ACTION:

○ ○ ○ ○ ○

○ ○ ○ ○ ○

REWARD

NAME: _____

THINK SHEET

WHAT HAPPENED:

HOW DID THAT MAKE YOU FEEL?

CONFIDENT	HAPPY	FRUSTRATED	PEACEFUL	SAD	WORRIED
LEFT OUT	ANGRY	ANXIOUS	SILLY	LOVED	EMBARRASED
IRRITATED	CALM	CONFUSED	UPSET	OVERWHELMED	_____

HOW DID THAT MAKE <u>OTHERS</u> FEEL?

CONFIDENT	HAPPY	FRUSTRATED	PEACEFUL	SAD	WORRIED
LEFT OUT	ANGRY	ANXIOUS	SILLY	LOVED	EMBARRASED
IRRITATED	CALM	CONFUSED	UPSET	OVERWHELMED	_____

Name: _____

NAME: _____

DRAW YOURSELF
↓

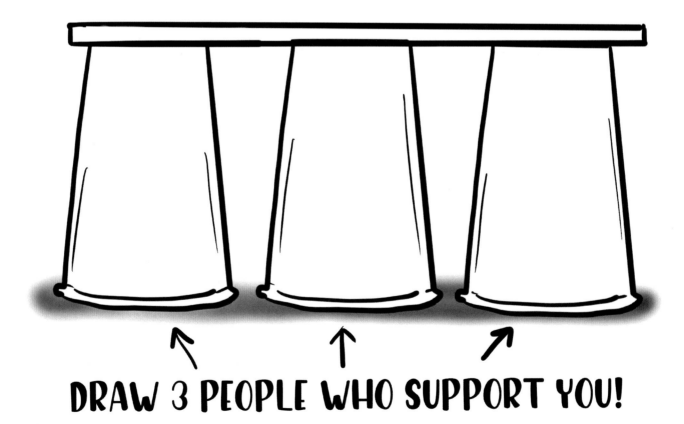

↑   ↑   ↗
DRAW 3 PEOPLE WHO SUPPORT YOU!

DID YOU MAKE A MISTAKE?
INSTEAD OF GETTING FRUSTRATED CAN YOU...

ERASE IT?

CHANGE IT?
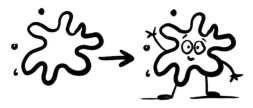

GLUE OVER IT?

COLOR OVER IT?

FLIP IT OVER?

Think like a PALM TREE!

NAME: _____

HOW CAN YOU SHOW RESPECT TO:

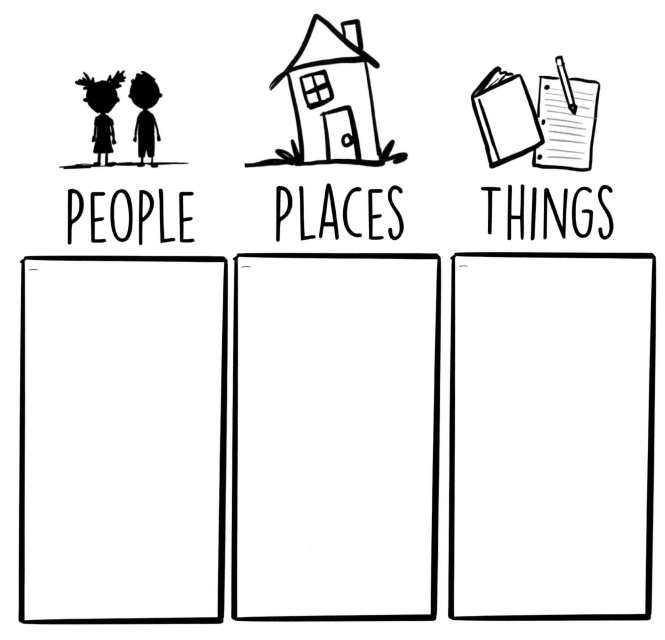

PEOPLE | PLACES | THINGS

NAME: _____

PERSPECTIVE

IS IT A HOUSE OR A CRAYON?

COLOR THE DRAWING AND WRITE YOUR ANSWER ON THE LINE BELOW:

_____

Finish The Picture

Use your imagination to turn this scribble into a drawing, then write a story about it!

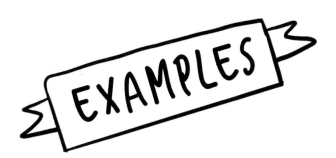

BEFORE

AFTER

BEFORE

AFTER

Finish The Picture

Use your imagination to turn this scribble into a drawing, then write a story about it!

Name:

SAFETY SIGNS AND THIER COLORS

Red: To tell you about HIGH DANGER that could happen quick.

Yellow: For caution, being aware of your surroundings, like to avoid tripping or falling.

Orange: For construction and warning tags.

Blue: Signs that label information about an item or area.

Black and White: For guiding traffic or telling people where to go.

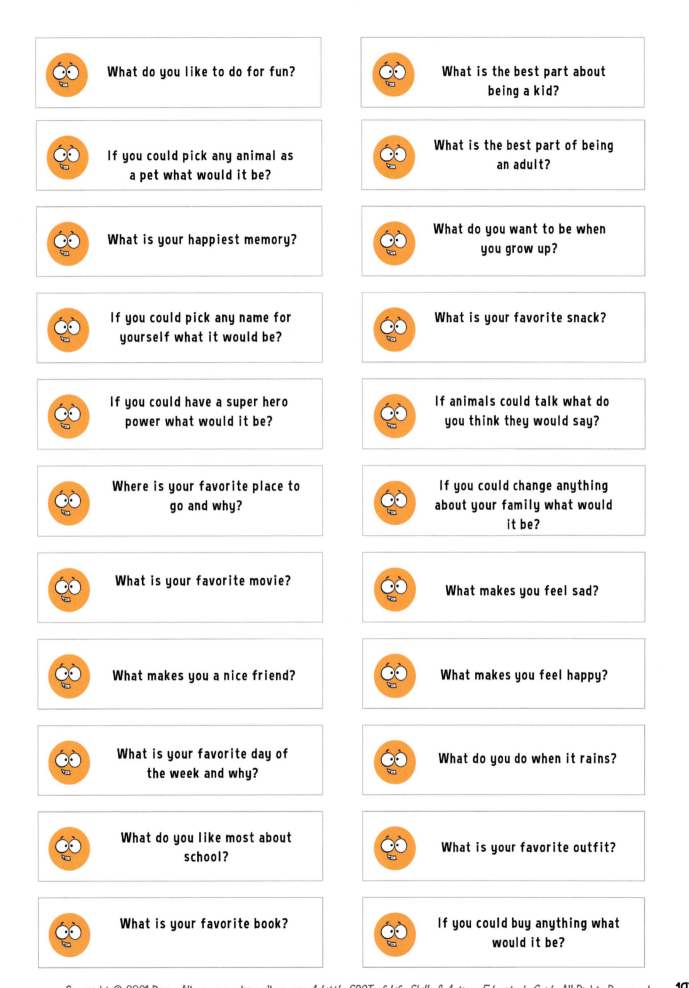

NAME:

WE MIGHT LOOK LIKE DIFFERENT LAMPS

BUT WE CAN ALL LIGHT UP A ROOM!

NOTES:

References:

CASEL SEL FRAMEWORK
https://casel.org/sel-framework/

COMMON CORE STANDARDS
http://www.corestandards.org/

Made in the USA
Monee, IL
14 September 2024